John Stevens

Sterling Silver 1

Englisch für Senioren

Cornelsen

Sterling Silver 1 – Englisch für Senioren

Verfasser: John Stevens, Bad Münstereifel
Beraterinnen: Britta Landermann, Steinhagen; Marion Karg, Schwäbisch Gmünd
Redaktion: Sigrid Janssen, Hannover
Redaktionelle Mitarbeit: Sarah Smith
Bildredaktion: Uta Hübner
Projektleitung: Helga Holtkamp
Illustration: Constanze Schargan, Berlin
Karten: Carlos Borrell, Berlin
Layout und technische Umsetzung: Typoly, Berlin
Umschlaggestaltung: Klein & Halm, Berlin

Außerdem sind zu diesem Lehrwerk erhältlich:
Audio-CDs ISBN 978-3-464-02007-4
Handreichungen für den Unterricht ISBN 978-3-464-02008-1

www.cornelsen.de

1. Auflage, 6. Druck 2013 / 06

Alle Drucke dieser Auflage sind inhaltlich unverändert
und können im Unterricht nebeneinander verwendet werden.

© 2005 Cornelsen Verlag, Berlin
© 2013 Cornelsen Schulverlag GmbH, Berlin

Das Werk und seine Teile sind urheberrechtlich geschützt.
Jede Nutzung in anderen als den gesetzlich zugelassenen Fällen bedarf
der vorherigen schriftlichen Einwilligung des Verlages.
Hinweis zu den §§ 46, 52 a UrhG: Weder das Werk noch seine Teile dürfen ohne eine
solche Einwilligung eingescannt und in ein Netzwerk eingestellt oder sonst öffentlich
zugänglich gemacht werden.
Dies gilt auch für Intranets von Schulen und sonstigen Bildungseinrichtungen.

Druck: Himmer AG, Augsburg

ISBN 978-3-464-02006-7

Inhalt gedruckt auf säurefreiem Papier aus nachhaltiger Forstwirtschaft.

Einleitung

Diese Einleitung gibt Ihnen einen kurzen Überblick über Ziele und Inhalte dieses Englischkurses.

Für wen ist *Sterling Silver 1* gedacht?
Sterling Silver ist ein Lehrwerk, das speziell für ältere Lernende entwickelt wurde. Mit „älteren" Lernenden bzw. „Senioren" im Sinne dieses Kurses sind alle Kursteilnehmer und -teilnehmerinnen ab der Lebensmitte gemeint, die über wenige oder gar keine Englischkenntnisse verfügen.
Der Kurs berücksichtigt die besonderen Bedürfnisse dieser Zielgruppe durch eine sorgfältige, sehr langsame Progression mit entsprechenden Wiederholungsschleifen, einer klaren Struktur und einer übersichtlichen Gestaltung. Inhaltlich befasst sich dieser Kurs mit Situationen, in denen Englisch benötigt werden könnte, z. B. auf Reisen, für Familien- oder Freundeskontakte.

Was wird gelernt?
Der Kurs vermittelt einen alltagsrelevanten Grundwortschatz von ca. 500 Vokabeln, eine Basisgrammatik (Schwerpunkt: Aussagen, Fragen und Verneinungen in der Gegenwart) und Redewendungen, die für wichtige Situationen benötigt werden: sich begrüßen und sich vorstellen, persönliche Informationen geben und erfragen (Name, Adresse, Telefonnummer, Familie, Freunde, Beruf, Tagesablauf, Freizeit, Vorlieben und Abneigungen), um etwas bitten, sich bedanken, sich entschuldigen, Speisen und Getränke anbieten, Einladungen aussprechen, Vorschläge und Komplimente machen.

Die mit diesem Symbol gekennzeichneten Texte sind auf den CDs.

Track 02

Wie ist *Sterling Silver 1* aufgebaut?
Dieses Buch erzählt eine fortlaufende Geschichte, die auf einem Kreuzfahrtschiff spielt (Näheres auf den Seiten 8 und 9). Nach jeweils vier der 20 Hauptlektionen gibt es eine **Wiederholungslektion**, also insgesamt 24 Lektionen (auf Englisch „**units**"). Ab Seite 100 finden Sie kurze Wiederholungsübungen zu jeder Unit, mit denen Sie sich allein zu Hause beschäftigen können. Jede der zwanzig **Hauptunits** ist gleich aufgebaut und besteht aus den Teilen *Presentation and Practice* (Musterdialoge, Wortschatz, Übungsdialoge), *Information & Tips* (deutschsprachige Hintergrundinformationen und Hinweise), *Grammar* (Grammatiktabellen und Erklärungen), *Useful Phrases* (englisch-deutsche Zusammenstellung der wichtigsten Redewendungen der Unit) und *Exercises* (Übungen). Nach jeder vierten Unit gibt es eine *Revision* (Wiederholung).
Im **Anhang** finden Sie zunächst *Home Practice* (zusätzliche Übungen zu den Units, die allein schriftlich zu Hause erledigt werden können), dann ein nach Units **chronologisch geordnetes Wörterverzeichnis** mit Übersetzungen der Musterdialoge. Den Abschluss bilden eine **englisch-deutsche alphabetische Liste aller Vokabeln** des Buches und die **Lösungsschlüssel**.
Die Musterdialoge der Hauptlektionen sind auf den **CDs** zu hören. Die CDs enthalten auch die wichtigen Redewendungen der Units, die Sie nachsprechen können.

Bevor Sie nun mit Unit 1 beginnen, werfen Sie einen kurzen Blick in das Inhaltsverzeichnis auf den Seiten 4 und 5 und lesen dann bitte die **Tipps zum Lernen** auf den Seiten 6 und 7. Danach, auf den Seiten 8 und 9, werden die Personen vorgestellt, die Sie durch das Buch begleiten.

Viel Spaß und Erfolg beim Englischlernen!

Inhalt

Tipps zum Lernen **S. 6**
The story **S. 8**

1 *Hello, my name's Ann* **S. 10**
Sich vorstellen • Jemanden fragen, woher er/sie kommt
Grammatik: I'm / You're / My name's • Are you …? – Yes, I am. / No, I'm not.

2 *I have a daughter in the United States* **S. 14**
Von der Familie erzählen
Grammatik: He's/She's • his/her

3 *Mary, this is Inge* **S. 18**
Jemanden vorstellen/ansprechen •
Nach dem Namen / den Sprachkenntnissen fragen
Grammatik: It's • This is • That's • your • Can you …? –
Yes, I can. / No, I'm afraid not.

4 *See you later* **S. 22**
Nach englischen Ausdrücken fragen • Sich verabschieden
Grammatik: What's …? • We are / They are • 's und of-Genitiv

5 *Revision* **S. 26**

6 *Good morning. How are you?* **S. 28**
Sich begrüßen • Fragen, wie es jemandem geht •
Etwas anbieten • Etwas bedauern
Grammatik: our • Is she …? – Yes, she is. / No, she isn't.

7 *Can I have the butter, please?* **S. 32**
Um etwas bitten • Fragen stellen und beantworten
Grammatik: Fragewörter • Fragen und Kurzantworten mit be • their • its

8 *How many are there?* **S. 36**
Fragen mit „wie viel" • Komplimente machen
Grammatik: Die Zahlen 1–24 • Die Mehrzahl von Hauptwörtern

9 *Where are you from in Germany?* **S. 40**
Die Lage des Wohnortes beschreiben
Grammatik: Verneinung von be

10 *Revision* **S. 44**

11 *What is there to do and see?* **S. 46**
Jemandem von seiner Stadt erzählen
Grammatik: there is/are • some • any

12 *Would you like to see some photos?* **S. 50**
Über Freizeitangebote sprechen • Einladungen und Angebote
Grammatik: Is/Are there …? • Fragen mit some/any • Would you like …?

13 *Tell me about your family* **S. 54**
Von der Familie erzählen
Grammatik: have/has

14 *Excuse me, what time is it, please?* **S. 58**
Nach der Uhrzeit fragen
Grammatik: Uhrzeiten • will

15 *Revision* **S. 62**

16 *It's lovely to get up late!* **S. 64**
Über Gewohnheiten sprechen • Seinen Tagesablauf beschreiben
Grammatik: Einfache Gegenwart • Satzstellung von Häufigkeitsadverbien/
Zeitbestimmungen

17 *I don't often eat a big breakfast* **S. 68**
Über Mahlzeiten sprechen
Grammatik: Verneinung mit don't

18 *Tell me about your son* **S. 72**
Über das Leben einer anderen Person sprechen
Grammatik: Einfache Gegenwart: 3. Person

19 *What's the weather like in Madeira?* **S. 76**
Über das Wetter sprechen • Vorschläge machen
Grammatik: Verneinung mit doesn't

20 *Revision* **S. 80**

21 *Do they speak English here?* **S. 82**
Fragen und Antworten
Grammatik: Fragen und Kurzantworten mit do

22 *Does she speak English?* **S. 86**
Über die Familie sprechen • Bilder zeigen
Grammatik: Fragen und Kurzantworten mit does • me/you/him/her/us/you/them

23 *I'm sorry. – That's all right.* **S. 90**
Sich entschuldigen • Erzählen, was jemand gerade tut
Grammatik: Verlaufsform der Gegenwart

24 *Goodbye* **S. 94**
Die Adresse/Telefonnummer erfragen • Sich verabschieden • Jemanden einladen
Grammatik: das Alphabet

25 *Revision* **S. 98**

Home Practice **S. 100**
Wörterverzeichnis nach Units **S. 109**
Wörterverzeichnis alphabetisch **S. 121**
Lösungsschlüssel Units **S. 127**
Lösungsschlüssel Home Practice **S. 134**

Tipps zum Lernen

Sie haben sich entschlossen, etwas Neues zu lernen. Das ist ein erster, wichtiger Schritt. Etwas, das wir aktiv angehen, gelingt uns immer besser als etwas, zu dem wir gezwungen werden.
Vielleicht ist es aber lange her, dass Sie in einem Klassenraum gesessen und sich in eine schulische Lernsituation begeben haben. Das kann Gefühle der Unsicherheit hervorrufen. Vielleicht befürchten Sie, dass Ihnen das Lernen schwer fallen wird oder der Kurs zu schnell vorangehen könnte. Solche Befürchtungen sind verständlich – aber unbegründet. Zum einen, weil dieser Kurs so angelegt ist, dass niemand überfordert wird. Zum anderen, weil Sie durch Anwendung konkreter Techniken und Tipps den Lernprozess bewusst so steuern können, dass er erfolgreich verläuft.
In diesem Abschnitt des Buches sollen einige dieser Techniken und Tipps beschrieben werden.

Goldene Regel 1
Regelmäßig und kurz üben
Gewöhnlich finden Sprachkurse für Erwachsene ein- bis zweimal die Woche statt. Diese Bedingungen sind nicht optimal, denn Pausen von mehreren Tagen zwischen Kursstunden führen zwangsläufig zum Vergessen – auch bei jungen Lernenden. Darum ist es wichtig, dass Sie zwischen den Kursstunden wiederholen. Und hier gilt die Devise: lieber regelmäßig und kurz als selten und viel. Kurze Lern- und Wiederholungsphasen sind effektiver. Es bringt viel mehr, täglich fünf bis fünfzehn Minuten lang die vergangene Kursstunde zu wiederholen, als z. B. einmal die Woche eine oder anderthalb Stunden zu lernen. Am besten ist es natürlich, wenn man regelmäßig täglich zur gleichen Zeit eine kurze Übungsphase einplant. Wenn Ihnen das nicht möglich ist, versuchen Sie sich einen Wochenplan zu erstellen, in den Sie feste Lernzeiten einplanen.
Übrigens ist es oft lustiger, mit anderen zusammen zu lernen. Vielleicht finden Sie Kursmitglieder, mit denen Sie sich außerhalb der Kursstunde verabreden können.

Goldene Regel 2
Entspannung fördert das Lernen
Eine wichtige Voraussetzung für das erfolgreiche Lernen ist, dass Sie nicht unter Stress stehen, sondern entspannt sind. Gönnen Sie sich deshalb vor dem Lernen eine fünfminütige Entspannungspause. Setzen oder legen Sie sich bequem hin, lassen Sie vielleicht dabei eine dezente Lieblingsmusik im Hintergrund spielen, schließen Sie die Augen und stellen Sie sich vor, Sie seien auf dem Kreuzfahrtschiff, auf dem unsere Geschichte spielt. Sie sitzen im Liegestuhl an Deck, Sie spüren die warme Sonne auf Ihrer Haut, eine leichte Brise in den Haaren, das Schiff neigt sich in den sanften Wellen.

Goldene Regel 3
Keine Angst vor Fehlern
Ein Sprichwort sagt, dass man aus Fehlern lernt. Und das stimmt. Haben Sie mal beobachtet, wie ein Kleinkind die Muttersprache lernt und wie oft es dabei Fehler macht? Sie sehen, Fehler machen gehört beim Erlernen einer Sprache dazu.
In der Schule wurden und werden Fehler oft als Fehlleistungen bewertet. In Ihrem Kurs ist das nicht der Fall. Machen Sie sich klar, dass sie eine wichtige Hilfe im Lernprozess darstellen. Im Englischen heißt es doch beruhigenderweise Nobody is perfect (Niemand ist perfekt).

Tipp 1
Wie trainiere ich eine gute Aussprache?

Die Aussprache ist ein Lerngebiet, in dem jüngere Lernende im Vorteil sind. Mit zunehmendem Alter fällt es schwerer, die Laute einer fremden Sprache nachzuahmen. Deshalb ist es besonders wichtig, gezielt diesen Lernbereich zu üben. Es gibt dafür noch einen weiteren Grund: Aussprache- und Intonationsfehler (d. h. eine falsche Satzmelodie oder Satzbetonung) können die Verständigung mit anderen stärker beeinträchtigen als z. B. Grammatikfehler.

Sie sollten möglichst viel mit der CD arbeiten. Hören Sie immer wieder die gesprochenen Dialoge, die Aussprache prägt sich dann leichter ein.

Wenn Sie mit dem Text soweit vertraut sind, versuchen Sie mit den Sprechern auf der CD mitzusprechen. Sie können auch die Pausentaste benutzen und die Sätze einzeln nachsprechen.

Die Arbeit mit der CD ist die wichtigste, die Sie alleine zu Hause machen können.

Tipp 2
Wie lerne ich den Wortschatz und behalte ihn auch?

Viele machen die Erfahrung, dass sie mit fortschreitendem Alter vergesslicher werden und Gelerntes weniger leicht behalten können. Deshalb hier einige konkrete Hinweise zum Vokabellernen:
1) Versuchen Sie Wörter nicht einzeln, sondern als Teil eines Satzes bzw. einer Redewendung zu lernen. Dadurch prägen sie sich besser ein und Sie lernen gleichzeitig, wie das entsprechende Wort verwendet wird.
2) Versuchen Sie „mit allen Sinnen" zu lernen. Es ist es wichtig, möglichst viele Verbindungen zwischem Neuem und Bekanntem zu schaffen.

Aber was heißt genau „mit allen Sinnen lernen"? Das bedeutet, dass Sie gleichzeitig das neue Wort lesen und sprechen und darüber hinaus versuchen, mit der Vokabel möglichst viele Bewegungen und Fantasiebilder zu verknüpfen.
Zwei Beispiele:
– Sie wollen in Unit 1 die Redewendung Nice to meet you (Nett, Sie kennen zu lernen) lernen. Sie lesen den Satz im Wörterverzeichnis, sprechen ihn laut aus und machen dabei eine Bewegung, als würden Sie jemandem die Hand schütteln.
– Das Wort juice (Unit 7) bedeutet „Saft". Stellen Sie sich vor, während Sie dieses Wort mehrmals vor sich hin sprechen, dass Sie eine Apfelsine auspressen. Spüren Sie, wie die Frucht unter dem Druck Ihrer Finger nachgibt. Vielleicht hören Sie sogar die Tropfen fallen und schmecken den frisch gepressten Saft auf der Zunge.

Tipp 3
Wie lerne ich Grammatik, sodass ich sie richtig anwenden kann?

Lange Zeit wurde die Grammatik als Hauptinhalt des Sprachenlernens angesehen. In diesem Kurs hat sie eine dienende Funktion: Im Mittelpunkt steht immer die Verständigung mit anderen Menschen. Dass Sie andere Menschen begrüßen, um etwas bitten, zu etwas einladen können, ist viel wichtiger als grammatische Bezeichnungen oder Regeln auswendig zu können.
Lernen Sie die Grammatik durch Anwendung. Prägen Sie sich Mustersätze aus den Dialogen ein, sprechen Sie sie nach, schreiben Sie sie auf. Wiederholen Sie die Übungen, bis Sie alles richtig können, ohne bei den Grammatiktabellen oder im Schlüssel nachzusehen.

Übung macht den Meister!

The story

In diesem Buch begleiten Sie Inge Schmitz aus Euskirchen bei Köln auf einer Reise in den Frühling. Jedes Jahr fährt sie mit ihrem Mann Bruno in Urlaub, meistens ans Mittelmeer. In diesem Jahr haben sie etwas Besonderes vor: Sie machen mit Brunos Bowlingverein eine lang geplante Kreuzfahrt zu schönen Inseln im Ostatlantik.

An Bord sind Reisende aus verschiedenen europäischen Ländern, unter anderem auch aus Großbritannien. Bald lernt Inge Schmitz die Engländerin Ann Thomas kennen, die aus Oxford stammt, der berühmten Universitätsstadt nordwestlich von London.

Inge und Bruno Schmitz

Schnell entdecken Inge und Ann Gemeinsamkeiten. Ann (Mitte 50) hat einen Sohn, der in Ebersberg bei München lebt, Inge (Anfang 50) eine Tochter in den USA. Dies ist auch der Grund, warum Inge und Bruno schon seit einigen Jahren fleißig Englisch lernen: Sie wollen sich mit ihrem Schwiegersohn, dessen Familie und den späteren Enkelkindern verständigen können. Inge lernt ganz konsequent und kann schon gut Englisch sprechen. Die gemeinsame Zeit mit Ann auf dem Schiff ist eine gute Gelegenheit für sie, ihr Englisch zu üben.

Ann ist geschieden und reist mit einer guten Bekannten, der 68-jährigen Mary Barnes. Mary ist Mutter und mehrfache Großmutter, hat aber vor nicht sehr langer Zeit ihren Mann verloren. Sie hat eine schwere Zeit hinter sich; jetzt ist sie dabei, sich auf ihr Leben allein einzurichten. Zunächst wollte sie gar nicht mitfahren, doch schließlich freut sie sich, dass sie sich von Ann überreden lassen hat.

Ann Thomas *Mary Barnes*

1 Hello, my name's Ann

Presentation

Track 02

1a Ann stellt sich vor.
ANN   Hello, my name's Ann, Ann Thomas.
INGE Nice to meet you, Ann. My name's Inge, Inge Schmitz.
ANN   Nice to meet you.

Track 03

2a Ann fragt Inge, woher sie kommt.
ANN   Where are you from, Inge?
INGE I'm from Germany.
ANN   And where in Germany?
INGE Euskirchen. That's near Cologne.

Practice

1b Stellen Sie sich den anderen Kursmitgliedern vor.
A Hello, my name's *(Karin, Karin Hermes)*.
B Nice to meet you, *(Karin)*. My name's *(Rolf, Rolf Schneider)*.
A Nice to meet you.

2b Üben Sie zu sagen, woher Sie kommen.
A Where are you from?
B I'm from *(Germany)*.
A And where in *(Germany)*?
B *(Schwerte. That's near Dortmund.)*

Zusatzwortschatz

Austria	Österreich	Berlin	Berlin
Switzerland	die Schweiz	Vienna	Wien
Munich	München	Zurich	Zürich

Presentation

Track 04

3a **Inge fragt Ann, woher sie kommt.**
INGE And you, Ann?
Are you from England?
ANN Yes, that's right.
INGE And where in England?
Are you from London?
ANN No, I'm not from London.
I'm from Oxford.

Zusatzwortschatz

the USA	die USA	France	Frankreich
Australia	Australien	Spain	Spanien
Canada	Kanada	Italy	Italien

Practice

3b **Fragen Sie ein anderes Kursmitglied.**
A Are you from *(Germany)*?
B Yes, that's right. / No, I'm not from *(Germany)*. I'm from …

Germany • Austria • France • Switzerland • Berlin • Munich • Cologne • Spain

Track 05

4 Hören Sie nun den gesamten Dialog.

Information & Tips

Vornamen
Briten, Amerikaner und Menschen aus anderen englischsprachigen Ländern gebrauchen sehr oft und schnell Vornamen, auch im Geschäftsleben. Dies bedeutet aber nicht, dass man „per Du" oder befreundet ist.

Sich die Hand geben
Briten und Amerikaner begrüßen sich oft (aber nicht immer) beim Kennenlernen mit Handschlag. Wenn man sich schon kennt, gibt man sich in der Regel nur vor oder nach einer längeren Abwesenheit die Hand.

England und Amerika
Im Deutschen sagen wir oft „England", meinen aber Großbritannien. Das stört die Engländer nicht – aber die Schotten, Waliser und Nordiren!
Schotten, Waliser und die Iren aus Nordirland haben alle die britische Nationalität, sind also British. Wenn man sie jedoch fragt, wo sie herkommen, sagen sie wahrscheinlich (Great) Britain, Scotland, Wales oder Northern Ireland – je nachdem –, nicht aber England!
Amerikaner bezeichnen sich als American (amerikanisch, Amerikaner/in), geben ihre Herkunft aber mit the United States, the States, the US oder the USA an.

Grammar

I'm from Germany. *Ich bin …*	**I'm not** from Britain. *Ich bin nicht …*	
You're from Britain. *Du bist / Ihr seid / Sie sind …*	**You're not** from Spain. *Du bist / Ihr seid / Sie sind nicht …*	💡 **you** entspricht „du", „ihr" und „Sie".
that**'s** right *das ist richtig*	that**'s not** right *das ist nicht richtig*	
Kurzform I'm you're my name's that's	**Langform** I **am** you **are** my name **is** that **is**	💡 **Kurzformen** werden meist in der gesprochenen Sprache gebraucht, **Langformen**, wenn man schreibt.

Useful Phrases

Track 06

Hello, my name's …	*Guten Tag. Ich heiße …*
Nice to meet you.	*Nett, Sie kennen zu lernen.*
Where are you from?	*Woher sind/kommen Sie?*
And you?	*Und Sie?*
I'm from Germany.	*Ich bin aus Deutschland.*
I'm from Berlin.	*Ich bin aus Berlin.*
Are you from England?	*Sind Sie aus England?*
Where in England?	*Wo in England?*
Yes, that's right.	*Ja, das ist richtig.*
No, …	*Nein, …*

Exercises

1 Zu welchem Bild auf Seite 13 gehört die Sprechblase?
   Schreiben Sie die Ziffern 1–4 in die leeren Sprechblasen.

1 Nice to meet you.

2 I'm from Stuttgart.

3 Yes, that's right.

4 No, I'm from Canada.

12 ◂ Unit 1

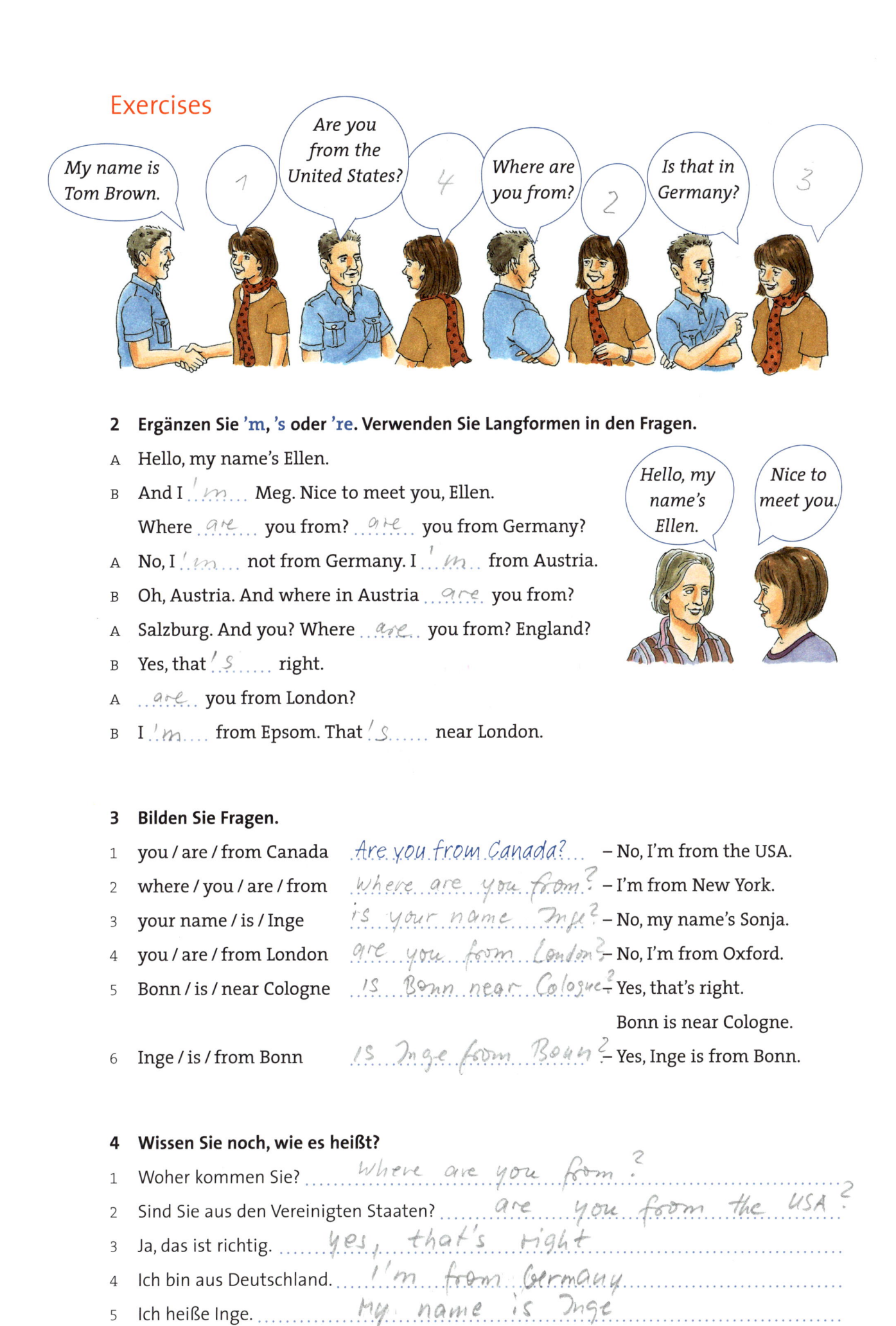

Exercises

Speech bubbles (in order): "My name is Tom Brown." — 1 — "Are you from the United States?" — 4 — "Where are you from?" — 2 — "Is that in Germany?" — 3

2 Ergänzen Sie 'm, 's oder 're. Verwenden Sie Langformen in den Fragen.

A Hello, my name's Ellen.
B And I '**m** Meg. Nice to meet you, Ellen. Where **are** you from? **Are** you from Germany?
A No, I '**m** not from Germany. I '**m** from Austria.
B Oh, Austria. And where in Austria **are** you from?
A Salzburg. And you? Where **are** you from? England?
B Yes, that'**s** right.
A **Are** you from London?
B I '**m** from Epsom. That'**s** near London.

Side bubbles: "Hello, my name's Ellen." / "Nice to meet you."

3 Bilden Sie Fragen.

1 you / are / from Canada — Are you from Canada? — No, I'm from the USA.
2 where / you / are / from — Where are you from? — I'm from New York.
3 your name / is / Inge — Is your name Inge? — No, my name's Sonja.
4 you / are / from London — Are you from London? — No, I'm from Oxford.
5 Bonn / is / near Cologne — Is Bonn near Cologne? — Yes, that's right. Bonn is near Cologne.
6 Inge / is / from Bonn — Is Inge from Bonn? — Yes, Inge is from Bonn.

4 Wissen Sie noch, wie es heißt?

1 Woher kommen Sie? — Where are you from?
2 Sind Sie aus den Vereinigten Staaten? — Are you from the USA?
3 Ja, das ist richtig. — Yes, that's right
4 Ich bin aus Deutschland. — I'm from Germany
5 Ich heiße Inge. — My name is Inge

2 I have a daughter in the United States

Presentation

Track 07

1a **Inge hat eine Tochter in den Vereinigten Staaten.**
INGE I have a daughter in the USA.
ANN   And I have a son in Germany!
INGE Really?
ANN   Yes.

Zusatzwortschatz

a grandson	ein Enkelsohn
a granddaughter	eine Enkeltochter
a brother	ein Bruder
a sister	eine Schwester
a cousin	ein Cousin, eine Cousine
a nephew, a niece	ein Neffe, eine Nichte
a godchild	ein Patenkind
a friend	ein Freund, eine Freundin; ein Bekannter, eine Bekannte

Practice

1b **Erzählen Sie über Ihre Familie.**
A I have a *(son)* (in Mainz).
   And I have a *(cousin)* (in England).
   And …
   And you?
B I have a …

14 ◂ Unit 2

Presentation

2a **Anns Sohn lebt bei München, Inges Tochter in Boston.**

ANN He's in Bavaria, near Munich.
INGE Oh yes.
ANN His wife is German.
And your daughter?
INGE She's in Boston.
Her husband is American.

Zusatzwortschatz

his girlfriend	seine Freundin
his partner	seine Partnerin
her boyfriend	ihr Freund
her partner	ihr Partner

3a **Ann will Inge ihrer Freundin Mary vorstellen.**

ANN Come and meet my friend.
She's over there.
Her name is Mary.

4 Hören Sie nun den gesamten Dialog.

Practice

2b Erzählen Sie von sich, zuerst von den männlichen Familienmitgliedern oder Bekannten.

A I have a *(son)*.
He's *(in Berlin)*.
His name is *(Bernd)*.
And you?
B ...

Erzählen Sie nun von den weiblichen Familienmitgliedern oder Bekannten.

A I have a *(daughter)*.
She's *(in Kassel)*.
Her name is *(Annette)*.

3b Fordern Sie Ihre Nachbarin / Ihren Nachbarn auf, in einem Rollenspiel ein anderes Kursmitglied kennen zu lernen.

A Come and meet *(Ingrid/Willi)*.
He's/She's over there.

Information & Tips

Wer ist mein Freund?

Ann will Inge ihrer Freundin Mary vorstellen. Friend kann im Englischen fast jede Person sein, mit der man einigermaßen bekannt ist und gut auskommt – ein enger Freund, eine gute Nachbarin, ein Bekannter, den man nur selten sieht. Briten und Amerikaner unterscheiden nicht zwischen „Freund" und „Bekannter".
Auch nicht zwischen „Freund" und „Freundin" – beides heißt schlicht friend.

Really?

Achten Sie auf die Art und Weise, wie Inge really und oh yes gebraucht und wie sie diese Wörter auf der CD spricht. Es klingt vielleicht ein bisschen übertrieben – aber nicht für englische Ohren. Unsere deutsche Sprechweise klingt für Englischsprechende manchmal etwas eintönig. Versuchen Sie also Inge nachzuahmen und sich insgesamt eine betont lebhafte Sprechweise anzugewöhnen.

Grammar

he	Bernd, my son, a brother
she	Ann, her granddaughter, a sister, my daughter

he er **she** sie
he und she werden für Personen gebraucht, nicht aber für Sachen.

I'm (I am) Ann.
You're (You are) from Britain.
He's (He is) my brother.
She's (She is) over there.

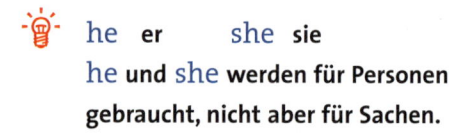

I'm	ich bin
you're	du bist, ihr seid, Sie sind
he's	er ist
she's	sie ist

I'm Ann.   **My** name is Ann.
He's Alan. **His** name is Alan.
She's Inge. **Her** name is Inge.

I	ich	my	mein/e
he	er	his	sein/e
she	sie	her	ihr/e

Useful Phrases

Track 11

I have a son / a daughter.	*Ich habe einen Sohn / eine Tochter.*
His/Her name is …	*Sein/Ihr Name ist …*
Come and meet my friend.	*Kommen Sie und lernen Sie meinen Freund / meine Freundin kennen.*
Really?	*Wirklich? / Ach ja?*

Exercises

1 Kreuzworträtsel crossword

1. She's his wife. He's her h __usband__.
2. I have a granddaughter Sally, and a g __randson__ Tony.
3. My co __usin__ is in America.
4. I'm from Bernau in G __ermany__.
5. I h __ave__ a son, Jack.
6. Not my brother, my s __ister__!
7. Not my sister, my b __rother__!
8. Come and meet my f __riend__ Mary.

9 __daughter__

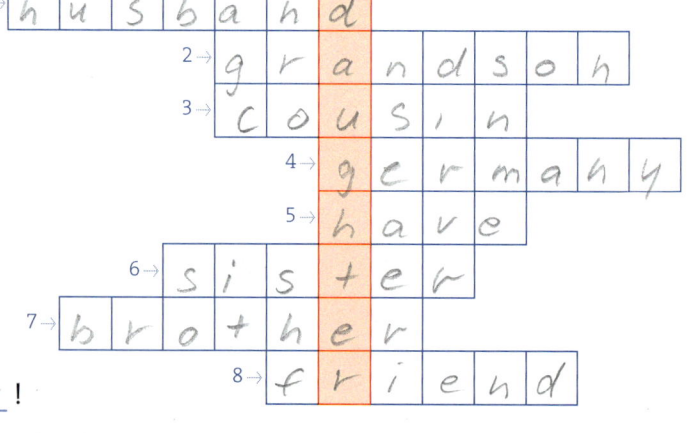

Crossword:
1→ husband
2→ grandson
3→ cousin
4→ germany
5→ have
6→ sister
7→ brother
8→ friend
9↓ daughter

16 ◂ Unit 2

Exercises

2 He oder she?

1. Ann Thomas — *she*
2. her friend Ann — *she*
3. her friend Mark — *he*
4. his daughter — *she*

3 He's oder his?

1. Come and meet my friend. *he's* over there.
2. *his* name is George West.
3. *he's* from Boston in the USA.
4. *his* daughter is in Germany.
5. George is my friend. *he's* nice.

4 He's, she's, his oder her?

- I have a daughter in Australia.
- Yes, *she's* in Sydney.
- Yes, *her* name is Lisa. *her* husband is from Switzerland.
- Yes, *He's* from Bern. *his* name is Urs.
- Oh yes?
- Sydney is nice.
- Really?

5 Wissen Sie noch, wie es heißt?

1. Ich habe eine Tochter in den USA.
   I have a daughter in the USA
2. Wirklich? *really*
3. Mein Sohn ist in Bayern, in der Nähe von München.
   My son is from Bavaria near Munich
4. Kommen Sie und lernen Sie meine Freundin Mary kennen.
   Come and meet my friend Mary

3 Mary, this is Inge

Presentation

1a Ann macht Inge mit ihrer Freundin Mary bekannt.

ANN Mary, this is Inge.
Inge, this is Mary.
INGE Nice to meet you, Mary.
MARY Hello.

2a Mary hat Inges Namen nicht richtig verstanden.

MARY Excuse me. What's your name?
INGE It's Inge.
MARY Inge. Is that right?
INGE Yes, that's right.

Practice

1b Stellen Sie zwei Kursmitglieder einander vor.

A (Karin), this is (Gerd).
  (Gerd), this is (Karin).
B Nice to meet you, (Karin).
C Hello, (Gerd). Nice to meet you to[o]

2b Fragen Sie ein anderes Kursmitglied nach seinem Namen usw.

A Excuse me. What's (your name)?
B It's …

your name • your first name • your surname • your address • the name of your town • the name of your street

Zusatzwortschatz

first name	Vorname
surname	Familienname
address	Adresse
the name of your town	der Name Ihrer Stadt
the name of your street	der Name Ihrer Straße

Presentation

3a **Inge fragt, ob Ann Deutsch spricht.**
Track 14
INGE Can you speak German, Ann?
ANN Yes, a little. *No, I cannot*
INGE Oh good!

Zusatzwortschatz

English	Englisch
French	Französisch
Italian	Italienisch
Spanish	Spanisch
No, I'm afraid not.	Nein, leider nicht.

Russian (Russchen)

Practice

3b **Fragen Sie ein anderes Kursmitglied, ob er/sie andere Sprachen spricht.**
A Can you speak *(English)*?
B Yes, I can. / Yes, a little. / No, I'm afraid not.

English • German • French • Italian • Spanish

Can you speak English? *Yes, a little.*

4 **Hören Sie nun den gesamten Dialog.**
Track 15

Information & Tips

Sich einander vorstellen

Wenn man vorgestellt wird, gibt man sich auch in englischsprachigen Ländern meist die Hand. Eine leichte Verbeugung ist aber nicht üblich und wirkt komisch oder altmodisch. Stattdessen lieber freundlich lächeln und dem Gegenüber in die Augen schauen. Wenn Sie zwei Personen einander vorstellen, gebrauchen Sie ruhig ihre Vornamen. Je nach Förmlichkeit der Situation können Sie auch den Nachnamen nennen. Beispiele: This is my wife Andrea oder This is Andrea oder This is Horst Schmidt. Etwas steif dagegen wirkt z. B. – auch in Geschäftssituationen – This is Mr/Mrs Schmidt (Das ist Herr/Frau Schmidt).
Genausowenig sollten Sie sich selber mit z. B. I'm Mr Schmidt vorstellen. Sagen Sie I'm Bernd bzw. I'm Bernd Schmidt (oder My name's …).
Im Englischen kann man sich nicht vorstellen, indem man nur den Nachnamen nennt (vgl. z. B. „Schmidt. Guten Tag.").

Can you speak German?

Mary kann kein Deutsch, aber Ann ist eine rühmliche Ausnahme – es gibt nicht viele Briten und Amerikaner, die gut Deutsch können. Deutsch ist an britischen Schulen normalerweise nur die zweite Fremdsprache (nach Französisch). Manche Briten und Amerikaner meinen (leider immer noch), sie brauchten keine Fremdsprachen zu lernen, weil ja alle Welt Englisch spricht. Vielleicht ist das aber auch der Grund, warum die meisten recht tolerant und hilfsbereit gegenüber Fremden sind, die Englisch sprechen, und Fehler einfach überhören. Nicht selten wird man mit einem Kompliment wie Your English is good für seine Bemühungen belohnt.
Also keine Scheu vor Fehlern, keine Hemmungen – munter drauflossprechen.

Grammar

It's (It is) Inge.
This is Mary.

That's (That is) right.
What's (What is) your name?

I'm Ann.   My name is Ann.
You're Mary.   Your name is Mary.
He's Alan.   His name is Alan.
She's Inge.   Her name is Inge.

Can you speak English? – Yes, I can.

it's	es ist
this is	dies ist
that's	das ist
what's	was ist

it entspricht „es", aber auch „er" und „sie", weil im Englischen alle Dinge sächlich sind. Zum „Tisch" oder „Baum" sagt man z. B. it, nicht he.

can   können

Useful Phrases

Track 16

This is Inge.	*Das ist Inge.*
Excuse me.	*Entschuldigung. / Entschuldigen Sie.*
What's your name?	*Wie ist Ihr Name?*
Can you speak German?	*Können/Sprechen Sie Deutsch?*
Yes, I can.	*Ja (kann ich).*
Yes, a little.	*Ja, ein wenig.*
No, I'm afraid not.	*Nein, leider nicht.*

Exercises

1 Ordnen Sie zu.

1 James, this is Helen.   D
2 Janet, this is Chris.   C
3 Excuse me. What's your surname?   A
4 Is Werner your first name?   E
5 Is Chur the name of your town?   B

A It's Müller. My first name is Barbara.
B Yes, that's right. It's in Switzerland.
C Nice to meet you, Chris.
D Helen, this is James.
E No, it's my surname.

2 Anna zeigt dieses Foto von ihrer Familie. Wie stellt Anna die Familie vor?

1. husband Charles
2. daughter Sonia
3. her husband Tony
4. grandson Philip
5. granddaughter Stella
6. son Kevin
7. son's girlfriend Carmen

This is my husband. His name is Charles. And this is …

Anna

crossword puzzel

3 Kreuzworträtsel. Um welche Sprachen handelt es sich?

1. Vive la France!
2. Auf Wiedersehen!
3. Bella Italia!
4. Olé!
5. Dinner for one!

1. FRENCH
2. GERMAN
3. ITALIAN
4. SPANISH

(5 ↓: ENGLISH)

4 Where's, What's oder It's?

1. *Where's* Vermont? – *It's* in the USA.
2. *What's* the name of your town? – *It's* Paderborn.
3. *Where's* Ann from? – She's from England.
4. *Where's* Bingen? – *it's* in Germany.
5. *What's* Calw? – *it's* the name of a town in Germany.

4 See you later

Presentation

1a Inge erzählt, dass sie mit ihrem Mann reist.

Track 17

INGE I'm here with my husband. We're here with his club. What's "Bowlingverein" in English, Ann?

ANN Bowling club.

Practice

1b Fragen Sie, wie Begriffe wie „Bowlingverein" auf Englisch heißen.

A Excuse me.
What's *(Bowlingverein)* in English?
B Bowling club.

Zusatzwortschatz

sports club	*Sportverein*	choir	*Chor*
hiking club	*Wanderverein*	English class	*Englischkurs*
German tour group	*deutsche Reisegruppe*	twin town	*Partnerstadt*
church	*Kirche*		

Presentation

2a **Mary will wissen, wie Inges Mann heißt.**

Track 18

INGE Well, we're here with my husband's bowling club.
ANN   My daughter-in-law is a member of a bowling club.
INGE Oh really!
MARY What's your husband's name, Inge?
INGE Bruno.

Zusatzwortschatz

neighbour	Nachbar, Nachbarin	teacher	Lehrer, Lehrerin
best friend	bester Freund, beste Freundin	son-in-law	Schwiegersohn

Practice

2b **Fragen Sie ein anderes Kursmitglied nach den Namen seiner Verwandten.**

A What's your *(husband's)* name?
B *(Werner.)*
A What's your *(granddaughter's)* name?
A …

2c **Finden Sie heraus, in welchen Vereinen Ihr/e Partner/in Mitglied ist.**

A Are you a member of a *(club)*?
B Yes, I am. / No, I'm not.
A *(What's the name of your club?)*
B …

3a **Ann, Inge und Mary verabschieden sich.**

Track 19

INGE Bruno is over there with his friends. They're all in the bar. I must go now.
ANN   OK. See you later.
INGE Yes, goodbye.
MARY Bye-bye, Inge.

Zusatzwortschatz

hotel	Hotel	restaurant	Restaurant
coach	(Reise-)Bus	museum	Museum

3b **Teilnehmer A ist mit einer Reisegruppe unterwegs und muss jetzt gehen.**

A I'm here with a German tour group. They're all in the *(bar)*. I must go now.
B Goodbye.
A Goodbye.

bar • coach • museum • restaurant • hotel

---

4 **Hören Sie nun den gesamten Dialog.**

Track 20

Information & Tips

Lokale

In Großbritannien bezeichnet das Wort **bar** den Schankraum in einer Gaststätte oder einem Hotel, bzw. den Tresen im Schankraum. „Bar" im Sinne von Nachtlokal heißt dagegen **night club**.

In den USA ist es wiederum etwas anders: Eine **bar** ist ein Lokal, in dem alkoholische Getränke ausgeschenkt werden.

Grammar

Kurzform	Langform
I'm	I am
you're	you are
he's	he is
she's	she is
it's	it is
we're	we are
you're	you are
they're	they are

What's Bruno's surname?
What's his wife's name?
What's your neighbour's name?
What's the name of his club?
What's the name of the restaurant?

Are you a member of a club? – **Yes, I am.**
Are you a member of a choir? – **No, I'm not.**

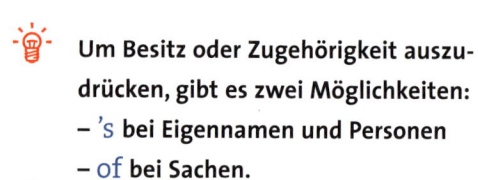

💡 Mit we are und they are haben Sie jetzt alle Gegenwartsformen des Verbs be (sein) gelernt.

💡 Um Besitz oder Zugehörigkeit auszudrücken, gibt es zwei Möglichkeiten:
– 's bei Eigennamen und Personen
– of bei Sachen.

💡 's um Besitz auszudrücken nicht mit 's = is verwechseln!

💡 yes oder no klingen als Antwort etwas schroff. Die Kurzantworten Yes, I am bzw. No, I'm not sind gefälliger.

Useful Phrases   *Nützliche Redewendungen*

Track 21

What's "Bowlingverein" in English?	*Wie heißt „Bowlingverein" auf Englisch?*
I'm a member of a choir.	*Ich bin Mitglied in einem Chor.*
What's your husband's name?	*Wie heißt Ihr Mann?*
I must go.	*Ich muss gehen.*
See you later.	*Bis später.*
Goodbye. / Bye-bye.	*Auf Wiedersehen. / Wiedersehen.*

Exercises

1 Am, is oder are?

I ..*am*..¹ Ann Thomas and this ..*is*..² Mary. She ..*is*..³ my friend. We ..*are*..⁴ from England. I have a son in Germany. He ..*is*..⁵ in Bavaria. Inge ..*is*..⁶ over there with her husband. They ..*are*..⁷ in the bar. Her husband's name ..*is*..⁸ Bruno.

2 Schauen Sie in die Wortliste auf Seite 109. Fragen Sie sich gegenseitig.

A What's … in English / German?
B It's …

Exercises

3 Schreiben Sie die Sätze unter das richtige Bild.

- She's his mother.
- They're grandfather and granddaughter.
- They're from Germany.
- He's her son.
- She's with her grandfather.
- He's from the USA.

They're grandfather and Granddaughter
She's with her grandfather
He's from the USA

She's his mother
They're from Germany
He's her son

4 Ordnen Sie den Fragen die richtigen Antworten zu.

1. What's your name? — A
2. What's the name of this restaurant? — E
3. What's his wife's name? — G
4. What's your surname? — C
5. What's the name of this town? — F
6. What's your son's name? — D
7. What's "neighbour" in German? — B

A It's Susanne.
B It's "Nachbar / Nachbarin".
C It's Schulz.
D It's Gerd.
E It's "Zum Goldenen Löwen".
F It's Einbeck.
G It's Friederike.

5 a Befragen Sie Ihre Kursleiterin / Ihren Kursleiter.

Sie/Er schreibt eine Liste ihrer/seiner Familienmitglieder an die Tafel (ohne deren Namen zu nennen).
Zum Beispiel:
I have … a husband / a son in Berlin / a daughter-in-law / a …

5 b Fragen Sie nach den Namen.

What's your *(husband's/wife's)* name?

son's / daughter's • son-in-law's / daughter-in-law's • grandson's / granddaughter's

5 c Zeichnen Sie zur Kontrolle den Familienstammbaum Ihrer Kursleiterin / Ihres Kursleiters – mit Namen.

5 Revision (Wiederholung)
Rewisdien

Wortschatz: Familienmitglieder
Arbeiten Sie in Gruppen zu dritt.

a Wie viele Wörter wissen Sie noch, die Familienmitglieder oder Verwandte bezeichnen? Schreiben Sie in Ihrer Gruppe eine Liste auf einen Zettel.

b Nacheinander nennt jede Gruppe ein Wort von ihrer Liste. Wenn ein Wort genannt wird, das Sie auch auf Ihrer Liste haben, haken Sie es ab. Ergänzen Sie Wörter, die nicht auf Ihrer Liste stehen. Welche Gruppe hatte die längste Liste?

brother, sister, cousin, nephew, niece

granddaughter, grandson, daughter, son, mother, father, grandmother, grandfather, Husband, wife, daughter-in-Low

Redewendungen: Andere vorstellen
Ordnen Sie die Sprechblasentexte in den Dialog ein.

INGE   Come and meet my husband.
       Ann, 4
       Bruno, 1
BRUNO 5, Ann.
ANN   2
INGE   Ann is from England.
BRUNO 3 in England, Ann?
ANN   From Oxford.

1 … this is Ann.
2 Nice to meet you, Bruno.
3 And where are you from …
4 … this is Bruno.
5 Nice to meet you …

Grammatik: Personen und Formen von be
Ordnen Sie zu.

1 Are you from the USA? — C
2 I have a son. — A
3 My friend's name is Jenny. — D
4 I'm here with my choir. — E
5 Are you from Germany? — B

A His name is Bernd.
B No, I'm not. I'm from Austria. *(austrian)*
C Yes, I am. From New York.
D She's over there.
E They're all in the hotel now.

Redewendungen: Sich und andere vorstellen

a Erfinden Sie für sich einen neuen Namen und Wohnort!

Name: Hilary
Town: Washington
Country: United States

b Üben Sie folgenden Dialog mit einem anderen Kursmitglied.

A Hello, my name's *(Hilary)*.
B Nice to meet you, *(Hilary)*.
   My name's *(Sophia)*.
A Nice to meet you, *(Sophia)*.
B Where are you from?
A I'm from *(Washington)* in *(the United States)*.
   And you?
B I'm from *(Rome)* in *(Italy)*.

c Gehen Sie nun in der Klasse herum und stellen Sie sich den anderen Kursmitgliedern vor.

d Machen Sie dann zwei andere Kursmitglieder miteinander bekannt.
(Mit ihren erfundenen Namen!)

A *(Hilary)*, come and meet *(George)*.
   (Hilary), this is *(George)*.
   (George), this is *(Hilary)*.
B Nice to meet you, *(George)*.
   Nice to meet you, too

Rückblick:

In den Units 1–4 haben Sie unter anderem gelernt, wie man …

… sich vorstellt.	Hello, my name is *(Ingrid)*.
… jemand anderen vorstellt.	This is *(Else)*.
… jemanden begrüßt.	Nice to meet you.
… nach der Herkunft fragt.	Where are you from?
… darauf antwortet.	I'm from *(Germany)*.
… über sich Auskunft gibt.	My first name is *(Ingrid)*.
	My surname is *(Mayer)*.
	My address is *(Lenzstraße 20 in Euskirchen)*.
	I'm a member of *(a choir)*.
	I can speak *(German and English)*.
… von seiner Familie erzählt.	I have a *(son)*. *(His)* name is *(Bernd)*. *(He's in Berlin)*.
	My *(husband's)* name is *(Klaus)*.
… sich verabschiedet.	Goodbye. / Bye-bye.

6 *Good morning. How are you?*

Presentation

1a **Ann fragt Inge und Bruno, wie es ihnen geht.**

Track 22

ANN   Good morning, Inge. How are you today?
INGE Fine, thanks.
ANN   And you, Bruno? How are you?
BRUNO Oh, OK. Too much beer last night, I'm afraid!

Practice

1b **Fragen Sie sich gegenseitig, wie es Ihnen geht.**

A   Good *(morning)*. How are you?
B   *(Fine, thanks.)* And you?
A   *(Fine, thanks.)*

Zusatzwortschatz

Good afternoon	*Guten Tag. [am Nachmittag]*
Good evening	*Guten Abend.*
Not so bad	*Geht so.*
I'm not very well	*Mir geht es nicht (sehr) gut.*

Presentation

2a   Ann bietet Kaffee an.

ANN   Would you like some coffee?
INGE Yes, please.
ANN   And you Bruno?
      Would you like some coffee?
BRUNO No, thank you.
ANN   Would you like some tea?
      Or water?
BRUNO Water, please.

Practice

2b   Bieten Sie einem anderen Kursmitglied etwas an.

A   Would you like some *(coffee)*?
B   Yes, please. / No, thank you.

coffee • tea • beer • water • wine • juice • milk

Zusatzwortschatz

wine	Wein
juice	Saft
milk	Milch

3a   Ann sagt, dass es Mary nicht gut geht.

INGE Where's Mary?
ANN   In our cabin.
INGE Oh. Is she OK?
ANN   No, she isn't, I'm afraid.
      She's not very well this morning.
INGE Oh, I'm sorry.

3b   Beantworten Sie Fragen mit Yes, she is oder No, she isn't.

A   Is *(Mary OK today)*?
B   Yes, she is. / No, she isn't.

Mary OK today • Inge OK today • (Karin) here today • (Ingrid) well • Mary a member of a bowling club • (Karin) a member of a bowling club • (Ingrid) a member of a … club

4   Hören Sie nun den gesamten Dialog.

Information & Tips

Wie geht's?

Auf die Frage nach dem Befinden erwartet ein Brite oder Amerikaner die Bestätigung, dass es einem gut geht (Fine, thanks). I'm not very well sagt man nur, wenn man sich richtig schlecht oder krank fühlt.

„Guten Nachmittag"

Eine von der Tageszeit unabhängige Begrüßung wie „Guten Tag" gibt es im Englischen nicht. Dafür gibt es je nach Tageszeit verschiedene Begrüßungsformeln: Good morning (morgens), Good afternoon (nachmittags), Good evening (abends). Wichtig ist noch, dass man Good evening nur sagen kann, wenn man sich trifft. Je nach Uhrzeit verabschiedet man sich abends mit Good-bye oder Good night (Gute Nacht).

Grammar

It's Mary's and my cabin. It's **our** cabin.

Is she from England? –
Yes, **she is**. / No, **she isn't**.

💡 unsere Kabine

💡 In der Kurzantwort werden das Verb (is) und die Person (she) aus der Frage wiederholt.

Useful Phrases

Track 26

How are you? – Fine, thanks.	Wie geht es dir/euch/Ihnen? – Gut, danke.
Would you like some coffee?	Möchtest du / Möchtet ihr / Möchten Sie etwas Kaffee?
Yes, please. / No, thank you.	Ja, gern. / Nein, danke.
She isn't very well.	Ihr geht es nicht gut.
I'm afraid not.	Leider nicht.
I'm sorry.	Es/Das tut mir Leid …

Exercises

1 **I'm afraid** oder **Excuse me**?

Excuse me. Are you David Barker?

No, *I'm afraid* not. David is in the restaurant.

Hello. My name's Julia Ford. I'm with the English choir.

Entschuldigung?

2 **Yes, she is** oder **No, she isn't**?

1. Is she Julia Ford? *Yes, she is*
2. Is she with a tour group? *No, she isn't*
3. Is she in Germany? *Yes, she is*
4. Is she from the USA? *No, she isn't*
5. Is she a member of a choir? *Yes, she is*

Exercises

3 Ein Ratespiel

Schreiben Sie den Namen einer Ihnen gut bekannten weiblichen Person auf und in welchem Verhältnis Sie zu ihr stehen.

Beispiele: *(Hannah), my granddaughter. / (Petra), my neighbour's daughter. / (Hannelore), my sister's granddaughter.*

Name der Person und wer sie ist:
Ilka, my sister's daughter

Ein Kursmitglied beginnt das Ratespiel, indem es nur den aufgeschriebenen Namen nennt. Die anderen Kursmitglieder müssen erraten, wer die Person ist, indem sie Fragen stellen. Die Fragen müssen mit Is ... beginnen und müssen mit Yes, she is oder No, she isn't beantwortet werden.

Beispiel: *Is ... (your neighbour)?*

best friend • sister • daughter • daughter-in-law?
son's girlfriend • son-in-law's / daughter-in-law's sister?
neighbour's granddaughter / daughter-in-law?
best friend's sister/granddaughter/daughter-in-law?
...?

4 Ordnen Sie die Sätze so, dass sich daraus ein Gespräch ergibt. Schreiben Sie die Ziffern 2–7 in die Kästchen.

- [3] I'm fine, thanks. And you?
- [7] Oh, I'm sorry.
- [1] Good morning.
- [4] Fine, thanks. Would you like some coffee?
- [2] Good morning. How are you today?
- [6] He isn't very well, I'm afraid. He's in the hotel.
- [5] Yes, please. How is your husband?

5 Wissen Sie noch, wie es heißt?

1. Wie geht es Ihnen? *How are you?*
2. Gut, danke. *fine, thanks*
3. Möchten Sie etwas Kaffee? – Ja, gerne. *Would you like some coffee?*
4. Möchten Sie etwas Tee? Oder Wasser? *would you like some Tea oder water?*
5. Nein, danke. *no, thank you*
6. Mir geht es nicht gut. *I'm not very well*
7. Ach, das tut mir Leid. *I'm afraid*

7 Can I have the butter, please?

Presentation

1a Bruno bittet um die Butter.
Track 27
BRUNO   Can I have the butter, please?
ANN   Yes, of course. Here you are.
BRUNO   Thank you.
ANN   You're welcome.

Zusatzwortschatz

sugar	Zucker
salt	Salz
pepper	Pfeffer
bread	Brot
toast	Toast(brot)
lemon	Zitrone
jam	Marmelade

Practice

1b Sie sitzen am Tisch. Bitten Sie um Speisen und Getränke.

A   Can I have the *(butter)*, please?
B   Yes, of course. Here you are.
A   Thank you.
B   You're welcome.

butter • milk • bread • coffee • water • sugar • tea • salt • pepper • toast • jam

---

2a Ann ist neugierig.
Track 28
ANN   Tell me. Who is the man over there? Is he in your bowling club?
BRUNO   No, he isn't.
INGE   He's very tired.
ANN   Yes, he is.

Zusatzwortschatz

tall	groß (gewachsen)	fat	dick
short	klein (gewachsen)	slim	schlank
athletic	sportlich	old	alt
good-looking	gut aussehend	young	jung

2b Beantworten Sie Fragen mit **Yes, he is** oder **No, he isn't**.

A   Is *(Bruno tired)*?
B   Yes, he is. / No, he isn't.

Bruno, tired • he, fit • he, young • he, tall • he, athletic • (Max), here today • (Max), tired

Presentation

3a **Ann ist immer noch neugierig.**

ANN And the people over there – are they in your club?
BRUNO Yes, they are.
INGE Their cabin is next to our cabin. Their name is Mayer.
ANN Are they married?
INGE No, they aren't. They're both single. They're brother and sister, Rolf and Trudi Mayer.

Practice

3b Beantworten Sie Fragen mit **Yes, they are** oder **No, they aren't**.

A Are *(Bruno and Inge married)*?
B Yes, they are. / No, they aren't.

- *Bruno and Inge married*
- *the Mayers from Germany*
- *the Mayers married*
- *they all in the restaurant*
- *(Karin and Alfons) here today*
- *(Ingrid and Frank) tired today*
- *the people in your … club nice*
- *the people here nice*

4 Hören Sie nun den gesamten Dialog.

Information & Tips

Höflichkeit ist groß geschrieben

Im Deutschen kann man höflich sein, ohne ständig „bitte" und „danke" zu sagen. Im Englischen dagegen ist es wichtig – wenn man nicht unangenehm auffallen will – immer please zu gebrauchen, wenn man um etwas bittet, und thank you, wenn jemand einem etwas gibt oder einen Gefallen tut.
Übrigens: Wenn Sie etwas mit „Danke" im Sinne von „Nein, danke" ablehnen wollen, achten Sie darauf, dass Sie im Englischen No, thank you, nicht einfach Thank you sagen. Beispiel: „Möchten Sie etwas Kaffee?" – „Danke." (Would you like some coffee? – No, thank you.)

„bitte"

„Bitte" entspricht please, wenn Sie um etwas bitten.
Wenn Sie jemandem etwas reichen und im Deutschen „bitte (schön/sehr)" sagen würden, können Sie im Englischen nicht please sagen. Richtig ist Here you are.
Wenn sich jemand bei Ihnen bedankt und Sie „bitte (schön/sehr)" im Sinne von „Keine Ursache" sagen wollen, verwenden Sie im Englischen You're welcome.

Unit 7 ▸ **33**

Grammar

Am I in this cabin?	Yes, you are. / No, you aren't (are not).
Are you tired?	Yes, I am. / No, I'm not (am not).
Is he in your club?	Yes, he is. / No, he isn't (is not).
Is she from England?	Yes, she is. / No, she isn't (is not).
Your book, is it old?	Yes, it is. / No, it isn't (is not).
Are we all here?	Yes, we are. / No, we aren't (are not).
Are you all in Bruno's club?	Yes, we are. / No, we aren't (are not).
Are they married?	Yes, they are. / No, they aren't (are not).

- In der Kurzantwort steht:
  - Yes + I am, you are, he is usw.
  - No + I am, you are, he is usw. + not.

- Die Kurzformen können nur in den Kurzantworten mit no, nicht aber in den Kurzantworten mit yes stehen.

I'm with **my** son.	We're with **our** friend.
You're in **your** cabin.	You're in **your** club.
He's in **his** cabin.	They're with **their** son.
She's in **her** hotel.	

- Zu den bisher gelernten kommt jetzt das letzte besitzanzeigende Fürwort its = „sein/e" bzw. „ihr/e" (bei Sachen).

- its nicht mit it's (it is) verwechseln:
  It's a hotel. Its name is the London Hotel.
  Es ist ein Hotel. Sein name ist...

wer
wo
was
wie

Who's the man over there? – He's my friend.
Where's he from? – Oxford.
What's his name? – Jack.
How is he? – Fine, thanks.

- who? = wer?   where? = wo/wohin?
  how? = wie?   what? = was/wie?

- who und where nicht verwechseln!

why = warum
with = welche / wessen
when = wann

Useful Phrases

Track 31

Can I have the butter, please?	*Kann ich bitte die Butter haben?*
Yes, of course. Here you are.	*Ja, natürlich. Bitte (schön).*
Tell me.	*Sagen Sie mal. / Sag mal.*
Thank you. – You're welcome.	*Danke. – Bitte (schön).*

Exercises

1a Ordnen Sie die Fragen den Antworten zu, indem Sie die Ziffern 2–4 in die Kästchen schreiben.

1 Is Ann's surname Thomas?   [2] No, they aren't.
2 Are Bruno and Inge from Hamburg?   [1] Yes, it is.
3 Is Inge's daughter in the USA?   [4] No, he isn't.
4 Is Ann's son in Cologne?   [3] Yes, she is.

Exercises

1b Schreiben Sie nun vier Fragen über andere Kursmitglieder.

Is your surname …? *Müller*   Is *(Hilde's)* daughter …? *married*
Are *(Karin and Hilde)* from …? *Spain*   Is *(Karin's)* son …? *young*

1c Stellen Sie, wenn alle fertig sind, Ihrer Kursleiterin / Ihrem Kursleiter die Fragen.

2 Schreiben Sie die Wörter unter das richtige Bild.

shop • bread • bar • butter • church • coffee • hotel • husband •
juice • member • milk • wife • neighbour • restaurant • museum •
salt • sugar • teacher • pepper • water • tea

People	Buildings	Food	Drinks
husband	shop	bread	coffee
member	church	butter	milk
wife	museum	salt	water
neighbour	bar	pepper	sugar
teacher	hotel	restaurant	tea
			juice

3 Wer ist wer? *(Teacher: see page 133)*

Tony Washington from London is in New York.
He's in the bar of the Plaza Hotel.

Die vier Personen unten sind alle mit Tony Washington
verwandt. Doch wer ist wer und wo halten sie sich auf?

MELANIE    TINA    GEORGE    HELEN

Stellen Sie Ihrer Kursleiterin / Ihrem Kursleiter Fragen und vervollständigen
Sie die Tabelle unten. So finden Sie heraus, wer wer ist.

What's … 's surname? • Who is he/she? • Where is … now?

First name	Surname	Who is it?	Where is he/she now?
MELANIE	Black	sister	restaurant in Oxford
TINA	Whistler	Tony's wife	museum in New York
GEORGE	Street	Tony's son in law	bar in Plaza Hotel
HELEN	Street	daughter	in the museum with her daughter

Unit 7 ▶ 35

8 How many are there?

sind dort / gibt es

Presentation

1a Ann will wissen, wie viele Mitglieder der Bowlingverein hat.

Track 32

ANN How many people are there in Bruno's club?

INGE Let me see. *Es gibt* There are one, two, three, four, five couples. *carpels (Paare)* That's ten people. The Mayers, twelve. Franz and Willi Günther, fourteen. And Irmgard and Ulla, sixteen.

ANN Sixteen people altogether?

INGE Yes, sixteen with husbands and wives and friends. Eight men and eight women. *(wimen)*

1 one	9 nine	17 seventeen
2 two	10 ten	18 eighteen
3 three	11 eleven	19 nineteen
4 four	12 twelve	20 twenty
5 five	13 thirteen	21 twenty-one
6 six	14 fourteen	22 twenty-two
7 seven	15 fifteen	23 twenty-three
8 eight	16 sixteen	24 twenty-four

Practice

1b Üben Sie die Zahlen.

A How many *(people)* are there in this class?

B …

people • men • women • friends • teachers • husbands • wives • married people • tall people • nice people

1c Spielen Sie Bingo. (Spielanleitung)

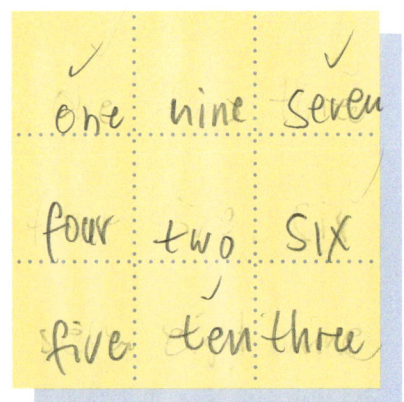

✓		✓
one	nine	seven
four	two	six
five	ten	three

36 ◂ Unit 8

Presentation

2a **Ann und Inge machen sich Komplimente.** *(Track 33)*

ANN   Your English is very good, Inge.
INGE That's nice of you to say so. Thank you. Bruno and I are members of an English class.
ANN   Is that an evening class?
INGE Yes, that's right. Our teacher is an Englishman.
ANN   Oh.

Practice

2b **Machen Sie sich gegenseitig Komplimente.**

A   Your *(accent)* is very good/nice.
B   Thank you. That's nice of you to say so.

Zusatzwortschatz

accent	Akzent
pronunciation	Aussprache
pullover	Pullover
watch	(Armband-)Uhr
blouse	Bluse
dress	Kleid

3 **Hören Sie nun den gesamten Dialog.** *(Track 34)*

Information & Tips

Bingo!

Bingo wird in Großbritannien als Glücksspiel, oft in ehemaligen Kinogebäuden und großen Hallen betrieben. Spieler (oftmals Spielerinnen) kaufen eine Karte mit einer Reihe von Zahlen darauf, z. B. zwischen 1 und 90. Die Zahlen werden in willkürlicher Reihenfolge ausgerufen bzw. erscheinen auf einer elektronischen Tafel. Wer zuerst alle Zahlen auf der Karte durchstreichen kann, hat gewonnen.

Bingo-Spielanleitung

Jedes Kursmitglied trägt mit Bleistift neun Zahlen zwischen 1 und 24 in beliebiger Reihenfolge in die Kästchen der Bingokarte ein. Der Kursleiter / Die Kursleiterin oder auch ein Kursmitglied ruft Zahlen zwischen 1 und 24 in beliebiger Reihenfolge aus. Streichen Sie die ausgerufenen Zahlen auf Ihrer Karte durch. Wer zuerst eine ganze Reihe senkrecht oder waagerecht durchstreichen konnte, ruft Bingo! Sie haben gewonnen.

Mann und Frau

Man (Mann) und husband (Ehemann), woman (Frau) und wife (Ehefrau) nicht verwechseln!
Das ist mein Mann. = This is my husband.
Wie geht es Ihrer Frau? = How is your wife?

Evening classes

Inge besucht einen Abendkurs. Abend- und Tageskurse für Erwachsene werden in Großbritannien in ähnlicher Art und Weise angeboten wie bei Volkshochschulen, kirchlichen Bildungsstätten und dergleichen Organisationen hier zu Lande. Das Angebot reicht von rein schulischen Fächern wie Mathematik über Sprachen zu Hobbykursen verschiedenster Art. Die Kurse finden in Schulen und Gemeindezentren statt.

Grammar

one friend	two friends
one couple	two couples
one teacher	two teachers
one class	two class**es**
one watch	two watch**es**
one church	two church**es**
one man	two **men**
one woman	two **women**
one wife	two **wives**
a class	**an** English class
the class	**the** English class

- Die Mehrzahl wird in der Regel durch Anhängen von -s gebildet.

- Bei Hauptwörtern, die auf s, ch, sh, x und o enden, wird -es angehängt. Dieses -es wird, außer nach o, wie das Wort is ausgesprochen.

- Einige wenige Hauptwörter haben eine besondere Mehrzahlform.

- Vor a, e, i, o, u wird a zu an und the wie three ohne das „r" gesprochen (wenn das u wie a gesprochen wird).

Useful Phrases

Track 35

How many are there?	Wie viele gibt es?
Let me see.	Lass/Lassen Sie mich mal sehen.
That's nice of you to say so.	Es ist nett von Ihnen, das zu sagen.

Exercises

1a Schreiben Sie die Zahl und die richtige Form des Hauptwortes aus.

1. I have (2 / grandson) _two grandsons_ and (3 / granddaughter) _three granddaughters_.
2. My wife has (2 / watch) _two watches_.
3. I'm a member of a club with (8 / man) _eight men_ and (7 / woman) _seven women_.
4. (3) _three_ of my (friend) _friends_ and their (wife) _wives_ are (member) _members_ of the club.
5. I'm in (2 / evening class) _two evening classes_, a German class and a Spanish class.
6. Can I have the (name) _names_ and (address) _addresses_ of (6 / hotel) _six hotels_ in the town, please?
7. I have (15 / pullover) _fifteen pullovers_ and (12 / blouse) _twelve blouses_.

Exercises

1b Nun schreiben Sie auf einen Zettel drei englische Sätze über sich selbst und lesen sie nach Aufforderung der Klasse vor.

Zum Beispiel: *Ich habe ... Kinder/Söhne/Töchter/Enkel/Enkelin.*
Wir haben ... Frauen und ... Männer in diesem Kurs.
In unserer Stadt haben wir ... Hotels / italienische Restaurants / ...

I have two sons.
We have two men in the kurses
In ours town we have some Hotels
(several)

2 A, an oder nichts?

1 I'm from ..an.. old town in Germany. It's ..a.. nice old town with ..an.. old church and ..—.. nice hotels.

2 My Italian class is ..a.. morning class, not ..an.. afternoon or ..an.. evening class. The teacher is ..an.. Italian woman.

3 Can you speak English? – ..a.. little. I'm ..a.. member of ..an.. English club.

4 My address? It's ..a.. German address, ..an.. address in Germany.

3a Schreiben Sie die Aufgaben und die Lösungen auf.

A 9 + 4 = *Nine and four is thirteen.*
B 10 + 12 = *ten and twelve is twenty-two*
C 7 + 4 = *seven and four is eleven*
D 15 + 5 = *fifteen and five is twenty*

3b Stellen Sie nacheinander je eine Aufgabe, die ein anderes Kursmitglied mündlich lösen muss.

Beispiel: Kursmitglied A: *Seven and eleven.*   Kursmitglied B: *Eighteen.*

4 Kreuzworträtsel

In diesem Kreuzworträtsel sind elf der zwölf Zahlen zwischen 1 und 12 versteckt.
Ergänzen Sie die Buchstaben, um herauszufinden, welche Zahl wo versteckt ist.

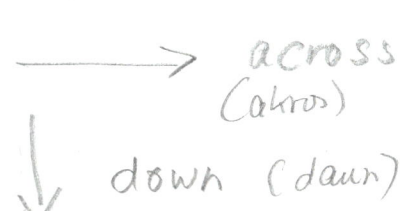

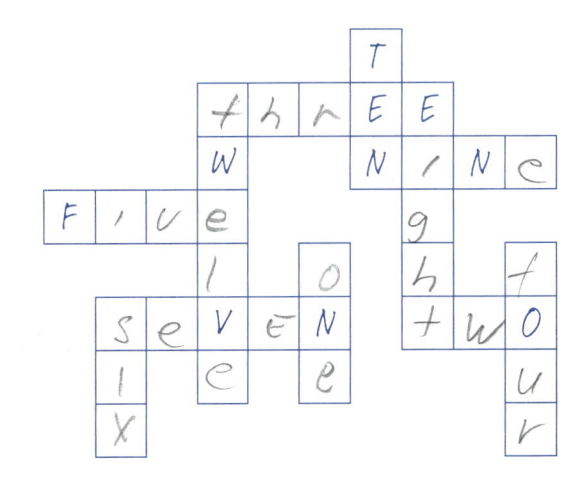

→ across (akros)
↓ down (daun)

9 Where are you from in Germany?

Presentation

1a Ann fragt, wo Inge und Bruno in Deutschland leben.

ANN Where are you from in Germany?
INGE We live in Euskirchen.
That's south-west of Cologne.
BRUNO It's a medium-sized town.
mittelgroße

Track 36

Zusatzwortschatz

north of	nördlich von
south of	südlich von
east of	östlich von
west of	westlich von
place	Ort
city	Großstadt
village	Dorf
big	groß
small	klein

nort
sans   sauf
*   iest*

Practice

1b Üben Sie zu sagen, wo Sie herkommen.
A Where are you from?
B I live in ...*Bernau*
(That's north/south/... of ...)
(It's a medium-sized town.)

That's north-east of Berlin
That's in the north of Berlin

square = Platz, Quadrat
Town = Kleinstadt (z.B. Bernau)

Capital city = Hauptstadt
border = Grenze

Presentation

2a Inge fragt, wo Anns Sohn lebt.
(Track 37)

INGE And your son, Ann?
ANN He lives in the south of Germany. In Ebersberg.
BRUNO Oh yes. That isn't far from Munich.
ANN That's right. It's about 30 kilometres east of Munich.

Zusatzwortschatz

in the north of	im Norden von
in the east of	im Osten von
in the west of	im Westen von
in the middle of	in der Mitte von

Practice

2b Sagen Sie, wo Ihre Verwandten und Freunde wohnen.

A And your *(son/daughter/sister/…)*?
B He/She lives in …
(That's in the north of Germany.)
(It's a small village.)
(It isn't far from …)
(It's about … kilometres from …)

30	thirty	70	seventy
40	forty	80	eighty
50	fifty	90	ninety
60	sixty	100	a/one hundred

3a Bruno sagt, dass sie nicht aus Euskirchen stammen.
(Track 38)

BRUNO We aren't from Euskirchen originally. I'm from Magdeburg originally.
ANN And you, Inge?
INGE I'm not from East Germany. I'm from Mannheim originally.

3b Was könnten Sie sagen? Verwenden Sie **isn't** und **aren't**.

Bruno isn't … • Inge isn't … • I'm not … • In this class we aren't (all) … • In Bruno's club they aren't (all) …

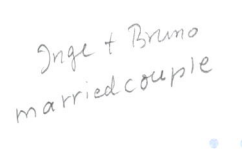

4 Hören Sie nun den gesamten Dialog.
(Track 39)

Information & Tips

big – tall
Big und tall nicht verwechseln: Beide entsprechen „groß". Big ist das allgemein gebrauchte Wort; tall bedeutet „groß (gewachsen)" bei Menschen, bzw. „hoch" bei Gebäuden.
Beispiele:
„Das ist eine große Stadt." That's a big town.
„Ihr Mann ist sehr groß." Her husband is very tall.

Kilometer
In Großbritannien und den USA werden Straßenentfernungen nicht in Kilometern, sondern in Meilen (miles) angegeben. Eine Meile ist etwa. 1,6 Kilometer. Das Wort kilometre wird in Großbritannien mit -re am Ende geschrieben, in den USA aber mit -er wie im Deutschen.

Grammar

Kurzform		Langform
I'm not	–	I am not married.
You're not	You aren't	You are not fat. *dick*
He's not	He isn't	He is not Italian.
She's not	She isn't	She is not my sister.
It's not	It isn't	It is not old.
We're not	We aren't	We are not tired.
You're not	You aren't	You are not old.
They're not	They aren't	They are not old.

I/We/You live near Cologne.
He/She lives in Berlin.

- Verneinte Sätze werden mit not (nicht) gebildet.
- Für alle Personen außer I gibt es zwei mögliche Kurzformen in der Verneinung.
- he, she, it – das „s" muss mit!

Useful Phrases

Track 40

Where are you from in Germany? — Woher in Deutschland kommen Sie?
I live in the north of Germany. — Ich lebe im Norden von Deutschland.
That's south-west of Cologne. — Das liegt südwestlich von Köln.
It's a medium-sized town. — Es ist eine mittelgroße Stadt.
That isn't far from Munich. — Das ist nicht weit von München.
It's about 30 kilometres east of Munich. — Es liegt etwa 30 Kilometer östlich von München.

Exercises

1 Beschreiben Sie die Lage der Orte auf der Karte.

1 *Oxford is about ninety kilometres north-west of London.*
2 St Albans *is about thirty-five kilometres* north-west of London.
3 Canterbury *is about eighty-five kilometres south-east of London*
4 Colchester *is about eighty kilometres north-east of London*
5 Guildford *is about forty-five kilometres south-west of London*
6 Henley *is about fifty-five kilometres west of London*
7 Brighton *is about seventy-five kilometres south of London*

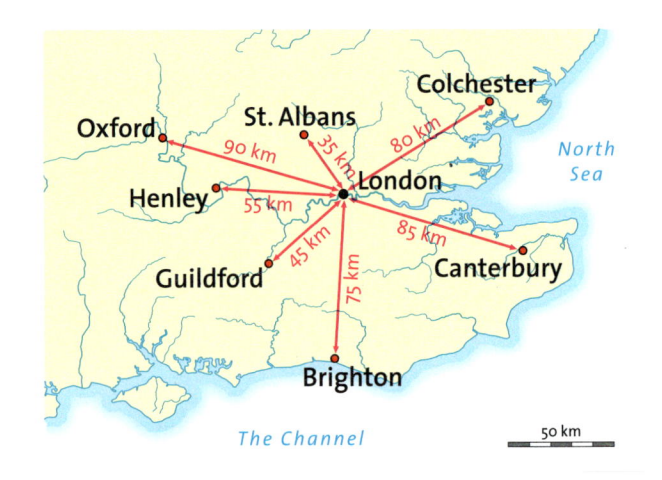

Exercises

2a Leserätsel: Woher kommt diese Person?

The place where I live is a city,
not a very big city.
It's not north of Colchester.
It's south-east of Oxford.
The place is under 100 kilometres
from London. We have a very
famous *(berühmt)* cathedral here.
The name of the place begins with C.

Canterbury

2b Und nun als Hausaufgabe:
Wählen Sie einen Ort in Deutschland, den alle gut kennen.
Schreiben Sie einen Rätseltext nach dem Muster oben.
Lesen Sie in der nächsten Stunde Ihren Text der Klasse
vor. Kann die Klasse Ihren Ort erraten?

3a Kreisen Sie die Zahl ein, die Ihre Kursleiterin / Ihr Kursleiter nennt.

A (16) 60
B 67 (76)
C (18) 80
D (57) 75

E 19 (90)
F 13 (30)
G (14) 44
H (15) 50

3b Schreiben Sie nun jeder eine Zahl auf einen Zettel.
Nennen Sie reihum Ihre Zahl und die anderen Kursmitglieder schreiben sie auf.

Birnau is a small town in the north of Berlin

4 Wissen Sie noch, wie es heißt?

1 Woher in Deutschland kommen Sie?
   Where are you from in Germany?

2 Wir wohnen in Euskirchen.
   We live in Euskirchen

3 Es ist eine mittelgroße Stadt.
   It is a medium-sized town

4 Es liegt etwa dreißig Kilometer östlich von München.
   It is about thirty kilometres east of Munich

5 Ich bin ursprünglich aus Mannheim.
   I am from Mannhein originally

10 Revision

Wortschatz: Essen und Trinken
Arbeiten Sie mit einem Partner / einer Partnerin.

Wie viele Wörter wissen Sie noch, die Speisen und Getränke bezeichnen?
Sehen Sie ggf. die Units 1–9 im Wortschatzanhang durch. Machen Sie eine Liste.
(Die Liste dient Ihnen als Unterlage für die nächste Übung.)

> coffee, tea, Fish, cheese, pumpkin, Tomato, carrot, fruit, Meat, milk, vegetable

Potato, Steak, Sup, Juice, Salt, Pepper, Onion, Pork, Chicken, Egg, Beer, Orange, Apple, Chocolat, Bread, Butter

Redewendungen: Am Tisch
Arbeiten Sie nun in zwei Paaren.

Jedes Paar hat die Liste aus der vorhergehenden Übung. Abwechselnd bittet jedes Paar um etwas, das auf der Liste steht.

A|B	Can I have the coffee, please?
C|D	Yes, of course. Here you are.
A|B	Thank you.
C|D	You're welcome.

Wenn das jeweils andere Paar die Speise oder das Getränk nicht auf der eigenen Liste stehen hat, bietet es etwas anderes an.

A|B	Can I have the coffee, please?
C|D	Sorry, we have no (*keinen*) coffee. Would you like some tea?
A|B	Yes, please. / No, thank you.

Grammatik: Die Zahlen
Alle Kursmitglieder arbeiten zusammen.

Ein Kursmitglied beginnt und sagt one. Der Reihe nach zählen die anderen weiter: two, three, four, five usw.
Wenn eine Zahl aus Versehen zweimal genannt oder sonst ein Fehler gemacht wird, beginnen Sie wieder bei one.
Wie weit können Sie zählen?

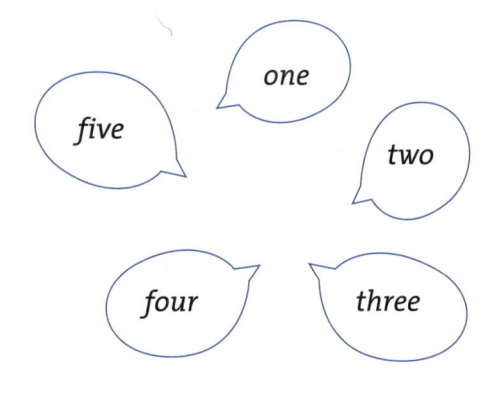

Redewendungen: Die Lage des Wohnorts beschreiben

a Jedes Kursmitglied erfindet einen neuen Wohnort.
Kreuzen Sie die Details Ihres neuen Wohnorts in dieser Tabelle an.

	1		2	3	4
in the	[X] north	of	[ ] England		
	[ ] south		[ ] France	[ ] small	[ ] village
	[ ] east		[ ] Germany	[ ] medium-sized	[ ] town
	[ ] west		[X] Italy	[X] big	[X] city
	[ ] middle		[ ] the USA		Mailand

b Üben Sie nun den folgenden Dialog mit anderen Kursmitgliedern.

A Where are you from?
B I'm from a place *(in the north of Italy)*.
A Is it a village, a town or a city?
B It's a *(medium-sized city)*.
   And you? Where are you from?
A …

· ·

Grammatik: Is he/she …? – Yes, he/she is. / No, he/she isn't.

Arbeiten Sie mit einem anderen Kursmitglied.
Wählen Sie eine Person, die Sie gut kennen, sagen Sie aber nicht, wer es ist.
Ihr/e Partner/in soll durch Fragen so viel über Ihre Person herausfinden wie möglich.

Is it a man or a woman?	Is he/she fat/slim?
Is he/she from *(Germany/Euskirchen/…)*?	Is he/she good-looking?
Is he/she young/old?	Is he/she a member of your family?
Is he/she tall/short?	Is it *(your son Uli)*?

· ·

Rückblick:

In den Units 6–9 haben Sie unter anderem gelernt, wie man …

… nach dem Befinden fragt.	How are you? – Fine, thanks. / Not so bad.
… etwas anbietet.	Would you like some *(tea)*? – Yes, please. / No, thank you.
… um etwas bittet.	Can I have the *(water)*, please? – Yes, of course. Here you are.
… sich bedankt.	Thank you. – You're welcome.
… Komplimente macht.	Your *(dress)* is very nice. – That's nice of you to say so.
… den Wohnort beschreibt.	I live in *(Paderborn)*. That's a place …

Außerdem haben Sie die Zahlen 1–100 gelernt.

11 What is there to do and see?

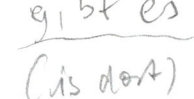

Presentation

1a **Ann möchte etwas mehr über Euskirchen wissen.**

Track 41

ANN Tell me about Euskirchen. What is there to do and see?

INGE There's a nice theatre. But there isn't really an interesting museum.

BRUNO There's a good bowling club! And there's the carnival, too. But there isn't a good football team.

INGE There isn't really a big park. But there's beautiful countryside near Euskirchen. The Eifel.

ANN Oh yes. The Eifel.

Practice

1b **Sagen Sie, was es in Ihrer Stadt/ Gegend zu sehen gibt.**

A What is there to do and see here in …?
B There's a/an …
 There isn't *(really)* a/an …

small • big • old • new • good • beautiful • nice • famous • interesting

park • cinema • theatre • sports centre • castle • river • church • museum

Zusatzwortschatz

a river	*ein Fluss*
a new swimming pool	*ein neues Schwimmbad*
a modern sports centre	*ein modernes Sportzentrum*
a cinema	*ein Kino*
a famous castle	*eine berühmte Burg, ein berühmtes Schloss*

Presentation

2a Bruno und Inge sehen die Vorzüge ihrer Stadt ganz unterschiedlich!

Track 42

ANN What else is there?
INGE There are some nice places near Euskirchen.
BRUNO There are some good pubs.
INGE There aren't a lot of good shops. But we're not far from Cologne and Bonn.
BRUNO There aren't any good night clubs.
INGE Oh, Bruno!

Zusatzwortschatz

| interesting old buildings | interessante alte Gebäude |
| nice old houses | schöne alte Häuser |

Practice

2b Was gibt es hier noch zu sehen?

A What else is there here in …?
B There are some …
There aren't any …
There are/aren't a lot of …

good • nice • old • interesting • new • big • beautiful

shops • restaurants/pubs • museums • buildings • places near here • houses • hotels

---

3 Hören Sie nun den gesamten Dialog.

Track 43

Information & Tips

Pubs

Bruno sagt, dass es in Euskirchen einige gute pubs gibt. Das britische pub ist eine besondere Einrichtung. Es ist oft in einem alten oder historischen Gebäude untergebracht. Und auch wenn das nicht der Fall ist, erinnert das Pub-Schild mit dem Pub-Namen draußen vor dem Haus oft an die Vergangenheit.

Die Räume sind z. T. mit alten Bildern, Messing- und Kupfergegenständen geschmückt. Manchmal brennt ein offenes Feuer im Kamin. Auf alle Fälle wird Wert auf eine gemütliche Atmosphäre gelegt; der Gast soll sich, oft wie in einem privaten Wohnzimmer, wohl fühlen. In den meisten pubs kann man heute nicht nur etwas zu trinken bekommen, sondern auch essen.

Eine Besonderheit gibt es dabei: Getränke und Essen werden an der Theke bestellt und gleich bezahlt. Das Essen wird zwar dann oft an den Tisch gebracht, sonst gibt es aber keine Bedienung.

Grammar

There's (There is) a good hotel.
Es gibt ein gutes Hotel.
There are a lot of good shops.
Es gibt viele gute Geschäfte.

There is **some** tea.
Es ist (etwas) Tee da.
There isn't **any** coffee.
Es ist kein Kaffee da.
There are **some** good pubs.
Es gibt ein paar gute Kneipen.
There aren't **any** clubs.
Es gibt keine Vereine.

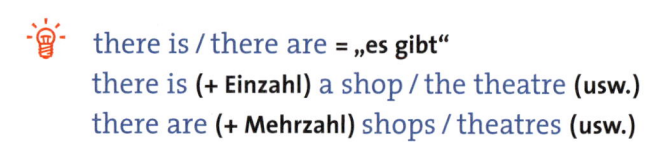

💡 there is / there are = „es gibt"
there is (+ **Einzahl**) a shop / the theatre (usw.)
there are (+ **Mehrzahl**) shops / theatres (usw.)

💡 some = „etwas / ein paar / einige"
not any = „kein/e"
In positiven Sätzen wird some **gebraucht,
in verneinten Sätzen** any.

in Fragesätzen auch any

Useful Phrases

Track 44

Tell me about Euskirchen. *Erzählen Sie mir von Euskirchen.*
What is there to do and see? *Was gibt es dort zu tun und zu sehen?*
There isn't really a good museum. *Es gibt eigentlich kein gutes Museum.*
What else is there? *Was gibt es (sonst) noch?*

Exercises

1 There is oder there are?

Ashford is a town in south-east England, about 100 kilometres south-east of London. It's an old town and *there are* ¹ some nice old buildings. *There is* ² an old church and *There is* ³ a museum, too. *There is* ⁴ a cinema in Ashford, and *There is* ⁵ (vierter) a theatre, too. *There are* ⁶ some nice shops and *There are* ⁷ some good hotels and restaurants. *There are* ⁸ some interesting places not far from the town, and *there is* ⁹ a beautiful old castle near Ashford, too.

Exercises

2 Was steht auf dem Frühstückstisch?

There is some ...

There isn't any ...

- bread any
- butter some
- coffee ~~some~~ any
- jam any
- juice any
- water any
- milk some
- sugar any
- tea some
- toast some

3 Kreuzworträtsel Crossword puzzle

1 Tell me a b o u t your town.
2 Is it far? – L e t me see.
3 There's a theatre, and there's a cinema, t o o .
4 There aren't a lot o f good shops.
5 I must g o now.
6 E x c u s e me. What's your name, please?
7 Nice t o meet you.
8 H o w many people are there in the tour group?
     wie viele
9 There's a museum, a castle and a theatre. And what e l s e is there?
10 There isn't r e a l l y a good hotel here.

1↓	2↓	3↓	4↓	5↓	6↓	7↓	8↓	9↓	10↓
A	L	T	O	G	E	T	H	E	R
b	e	o	f	o	x	o	o	L	e
o	t	o			c		w	s	a
u					u			e	l
t					s				l
					e				y

4 Wissen Sie noch, wie es heißt?

1 Erzählen Sie mir über Euskirchen.
   Tell me about Euskirchen

2 Was gibt es zu tun und zu sehen?
   What is there to do and see?

3 Was gibt es noch?
   What else is there?

4 Es gibt nicht viele gute Geschäfte.
   There aren't a lot of good shops.

5 Die Landschaft ist schön.
   The countryside is beautiful

12 Would you like to see some photos?

Presentation

1a **Bruno möchte etwas über Oxford wissen.**

BRUNO Tell me about Oxford.
Is there a good football team?
MARY No, there isn't. Sorry, Bruno.
ANN There's a football club, but it isn't very good.
BRUNO Is there a carnival?
ANN Yes, there is. But it isn't like the German carnival.

Practice

1b **Was gibt es in unserer Gegend/Stadt?**
A Is there (nice countryside near here)?
B Yes, there is. / No, there isn't.

- nice countryside near here
- a big sports centre in …
- a good restaurant/hotel in …
- an Italian restaurant in …
- a theatre in …
- an interesting museum in …
- a castle near here
- a famous building in …
- a big city near here

2a **Bruno möchte mehr wissen.**

BRUNO Are there any good pubs?
MARY Yes, there are.
BRUNO Are there a lot of night clubs?
ANN No, there aren't. Sorry, Bruno.
INGE Oxford is an old university town.
BRUNO Yes, I know, but ….

2b **Was für Leute gibt es in diesem Englischkurs?**
A Are there (a lot of women) in this class?
B Yes, there are. / No, there aren't.

a lot of women • many men • any people from east/west Germany • any people with friends in America • any people with a good English accent • any married couples • any young people • a lot of nice people

Presentation

3a Ann fragt, ob Inge und Bruno Fotos sehen möchten.

Track 47

ANN Would you like to see some photos?
INGE Yes, please.
MARY This is one of the old colleges.
INGE Oh lovely.

Practice

3b Fordern Sie ein anderes Kursmitglied auf, etwas mit Ihnen zu unternehmen.

A Would you like to *(go for a meal)*?
B Yes, please. / No, thank you. Later perhaps.

*go for a meal`• go for a drink now •
see the town • visit our museum •
go shopping • go to the cinema •
go to the theatre •
come and meet my family •
see the countryside near here*

Zusatzwortschatz

No, thank you. Later perhaps.	Nein, danke. Später vielleicht.
I'm sorry, but I can't just now.	Es tut mir Leid, aber ich kann gerade nicht.
go for a meal / go for a drink	essen gehen / etwas trinken gehen
go to the theatre/cinema	ins Theater/Kino gehen
go shopping	einkaufen gehen
visit my family	meine Familie besuchen

4 Hören Sie nun den gesamten Dialog.

Track 48

Information & Tips

Oxford und „Oxford-Englisch"

Oxford liegt etwa 90 Kilometer nordwestlich von London und ist ein beliebtes Reiseziel für Englandbesucher. In Oxford ist die älteste Universität Englands (aus dem 12. Jahrhundert) mit vielen herrlichen mittelalterlichen Gebäuden. Die Universität setzt sich aus verschiedenen Colleges zusammen; das sind quasi eigenständige Schulen innerhalb der Universität, wo Studenten und Lehrpersonal auch wohnen. Das berühmteste und sehenswerteste College ist Christ Church aus dem 15. Jahrhundert. Es liegt an der Themse.

Unter „Oxford-Englisch" versteht man teilweise hier zu Lande immer noch das „richtige", korrekte Englisch. Der Ausdruck ist aber veraltet und wurde sogar früher in England eher im negativen Sinn gebraucht, da Oxford English als affektiert und snobistisch galt.

Grammar

Is there a carnival?	Yes, **there is.**
	No, **there isn't.**
Are there any good hotels?	Yes, **there are.**
	No, **there aren't.**

💡 Fragen und Kurzantworten mit there is und there are werden wie andere Fragen und Kurzantworten mit is und are gebildet: Is bzw. are wird in der Kurzantwort wiederholt.

Would you like to see **some** photos?
Can I have **some** water, please?
Is there **any** wine?
Are there **any** good pubs?

💡 In Angeboten oder Bitten steht some. In anderen Fragen wird any gebraucht.

Would you like some coffee?
Would you like **to see** the town?

💡 would you like wird vor einem Verb mit to gebraucht.

Useful Phrases

Track 49

It isn't like the German carnival.	Es ist nicht wie der deutsche Karneval.
Would you like to see some photos?	Möchten Sie (einige) Fotos sehen?
Yes, please.	Ja, gerne.
Oh lovely.	Ach, schön!
No, thank you. Later perhaps.	Danke, nein. Später vielleicht.
I'm sorry, but I can't just now.	Es tut mir Leid, aber ich kann gerade nicht.

Exercises

1 Beantworten Sie diese Fragen zu dem Bild auf Seite 53 mit Yes, there is/are oder No, there isn't/aren't.

1. Is there an Englishman in the group? _Yes, there is_
2. Is there an Englishwoman in the group? _No, there isn't_
3. Is there a tall man? [groß] _Yes, there is_
4. Is there an Italian woman? _No, there isn't_
5. Are there any people from Switzerland? _Yes, there are_
6. Is there a teacher in the group? _Yes, there is_
7. Is there a Spanish man? _No, there isn't_
8. Are there any Germans? _No, there aren't_
9. Are there any married couples? _Yes, there are_

2 Bieten Sie jemandem etwas an.

Would you like some …
- tea?
- coffee?
- milk?
- water?
- juice?
- wine?
- beer?

- Yes, please.
- No, thank you.
- Later perhaps.
- Not just now, thank you.

**3 Ergänzen Sie die Fragen mit some oder any.
Danach wählen Sie die passende Antwort rechts.**

1 Can I have ...some... butter, please?
2 Are there ...any... good museums here?
3 Can I see ...any... (some) photos, please?
4 Would you like ...some... coffee?
5 Is there ...any... beer?
6 Are there ...any... Germans here?

[4] Yes, please.
[5] No, sorry. But there is some nice wine.
[1] Yes, of course. Here you are.
[6] No, I'm afraid not. We're all from Austria.
[2] No, there aren't, I'm afraid.
[3] Sorry. The photos are all in my hotel.

some
→ weil can - Frage

Unit 12 ▶ 53

13 Tell me about your family

Presentation

1a Inge fragt Mary nach ihrer Familie.
(Track 50)

INGE Mary, tell me about your family.
MARY Well, I have a son, John. He's married and has two daughters.
INGE Oh lovely.
MARY I also have a daughter. She's divorced. She has two boys.
INGE So you have four grandchildren.
MARY Yes, that's right.

Zusatzwortschatz

a child, two children	ein Kind, zwei Kinder
I have no children.	Ich habe keine Kinder.
relative	Verwandte(r)
girl	Mädchen

Practice

1b Unterhalten Sie sich über Ihre Familien.

A Tell me about your family.
B Well, I have … *(He/She has …)*

children • son • daughter • relatives • Verwandte
an English/American husband/wife •
boy • girl

Presentation

2a Mary erzählt über ihre Enkelkinder.
(Track 51)

INGE How old are your grandchildren?
MARY The two boys, Craig and Alexander, are twelve and nine. And my granddaughters are five and three.
INGE Oh nice.
MARY The children also have some animals. Craig and Alexander have a dog. And my son's family has a cat called Samson.
INGE That's a funny name for a cat.

3a Inge stellt fest, dass ihr Kaffee kalt ist.
(Track 52)

INGE This coffee's cold.
MARY Oh dear!
INGE Is your tea OK?
MARY Yes, it's fine.
INGE Oh good!

Zusatzwortschatz

(too) hot	(zu) heiß
warm	warm
awful	schrecklich
noisy	laut
late	(zu) spät, verspätet

Practice

2b Erzählen Sie Ihrem Nachbarn / Ihrer Nachbarin Näheres über Ihre Familie.

A *(My grandchildren are ten and eleven.)*
(Their names are …)
(I also have a cat called Lilly.)

2c Und nun erzählen Sie der Klasse, was Ihr/e Nachbar/in erzählt hat.

B *(Ingrid)* has *(two children)*.
(She also) has *(five grandchildren)*.

3b Sagen Sie, ob das, was Ihr/e Nachbar/in berichtet, Sie freut *(Oh good!)* oder Ihnen Leid tut *(Oh dear!)*.

A *(This coffee is cold)*.
B Oh good! / Oh dear!

This coffee is cold. • *And my beer is warm* • *There are some very nice shops here.* • *Our cabin is very hot.* • *The Boston is an awful hotel.* • *It's very noisy.* • *But the countryside near the town is lovely.* • *You're late!*

4 Hören Sie nun den gesamten Dialog.
(Track 53)

Information & Tips

warm und hot

Nicht warm, sondern hot ist manchmal die englische Entsprechung für das deutsche Wort „warm". So heißt es z. B.: It's hot in here. = Es ist warm (unangenehm warm) hier. I'm hot. = Mir ist warm (unangenehm warm). It's a hot meal. = Es ist eine warme Mahlzeit.

so und also

Das deutsche Wort „also" nicht mit dem englischen Wort also verwechseln! Inge sagt zu Mary So you have four grandchildren. (Sie haben also vier Enkelkinder.) Das deutsche Wort „also" heißt im Englischen so. Das englische Wort also hat die gleiche Bedeutung wie too, nämlich „auch": They also have some pets. (Sie haben auch Haustiere.)

Grammar

I	**have** a dog.
You	**have** four grandchildren.
He	**has** a son in Canada.
She	**has** a nice name.
It	**has** good beer.
We	**have** a cat.
You	**have** a good-looking son.
They	**have** two daughters.

💡 Von dem Verb be wissen Sie, dass es für die dritte Person (he/she/it) eine besondere Form gibt (is).

💡 Das Verb have ist ähnlich. Nach he/she/it heißt es nicht have, sondern has.

Useful Phrases

Track 54

Oh dear!	O je!
Oh good!	Gut!/Prima!
It's fine.	Er/Sie/Es ist gut so.
A cat called Samson.	Eine Katze namens Samson.

Exercises

1 Kreuzworträtsel

down ⬇ (senkrecht)

1. Are you from Munich? – Yes, I _am_.
2. My husband is _over_ there in the bar.
3. There are good pubs, and there's a good bowling club, _too_.
7. _one_, two, three
8. We're from a place _near_ London.
9. I'm here _with_ my husband.
10. There aren't a _lot_ of good shops.
13. That's interesting. But what _else_ can you tell me?

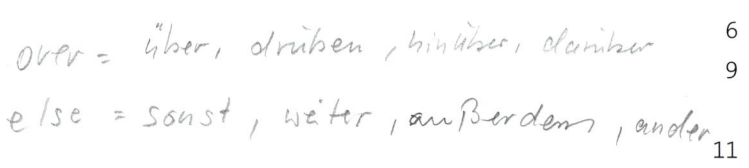

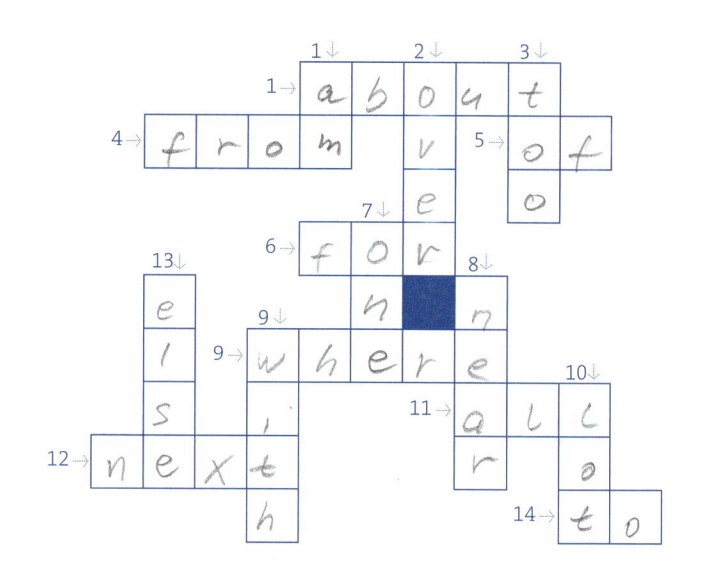

across ➡ (waagerecht)

1. Oxford is _about_ 90 kilometres north-west of London.
4. Her husband is _from_ France. He's French.
5. Ashford is south-east _of_ London.
6. That's a funny (lustiger) name _for_ a cat.
9. _Where_ are you from? – Germany.
11. _all_ my children live in Germany.
12. Their cabin is _next_ to our cabin.
14. Nice _to_ meet you.

over = über, drüben, hinüber, darüber
else = sonst, weiter, außerdem, ander

Exercises

2a Ein Spiel: Wahr oder unwahr?
Ein Kursmitglied macht eine Aussage über ein anderes nach folgendem Muster.
Die anderen müssen entscheiden, ob die Aussage wahr ist (true) oder unwahr (false).

(Werner) has a
- son / daughter / husband
- grandson / granddaughter
- son-in-law / daughter-in-law
- neighbour / friend
- cat / dog

called *(Bernd)*.
in *(America)*.

2b Und nun machen Sie nach diesem Muster weiter.

We/I have
- a restaurant / hotel called *(Azur)*
- a theatre / museum / cinema
- a university / a good football team
- a castle / a big sports centre
- a lot of …
- some …

near here.
here in *(Paderborn)*.

3 Ordnen Sie die Sätze so, dass sich daraus ein Gespräch ergibt.
Schreiben Sie die Ziffern 2–6 in die Kästchen.

[5] Yes, it is. My sister isn't very well just now.
[3] Near Vancouver.
[1] I have some relatives in Canada.
[2] Oh really? Where in Canada?
[4] Oh lovely. That's a beautiful city.
[6] Oh dear! I'm sorry.

4 Ordnen Sie die Begriffe in die richtige Gruppe ein.

wife • girl • children • boy • husband • couple *Ehepaar*

man *male (männlich)*	woman *female (weiblich)*	people
boy	wife	couple
husband	girl	children

5 Wissen Sie noch, wie es heißt?

1 Er ist verheiratet und hat zwei Kinder. *his is married and has two children*
2 Sie ist geschieden. *She is divored*
3 Wie alt sind Ihre Enkelkinder? *How old are your grandcildreen?*
4 Meine Enkeltöchter sind fünf und drei. *My granddaudhter are five and three years old.*

14 Excuse me, what time is it, please?

Presentation

1a   **Das Schiff macht Halt in Tanger.**
Track 55
ANN   Excuse me, what time is it, please?
MAN   It's 10 o'clock.
ANN   And when will we be in Tangier?
MAN   In one hour, at 11 o'clock.

Zusatzwortschatz
What is the time? *Wie spät ist es?*

2a   **Ann will wissen, wie lange die Passagiere in Tanger bleiben können.**
Track 56
ANN   And when will the ship leave again?
MAN   At half past seven.
ANN   So how much time will we have there?
MAN   Eight and a half hours.

Zusatzwortschatz
arrive   ankommen
plane   Flugzeug
train   Zug

Practice

1b   **A ist Reisende/r, B ist Reiseleiter/in.**
A   Excuse me, what time is it, please?
B   It's *(six)* o'clock.
A   And when will we be in *(London)*?
B   In one hour, at *(seven)* o'clock.

6.00 – London • 8.00 – Berlin •
11.00 – New York • 3.00 – Rome •
7.00 – San Francisco • 9.00 – Washington

2b   **Üben Sie die Uhrzeit mit half past.**
A   When will *(the plane leave Rome)*, please?
B   At half past *(ten)*.
A   Thank you.

- plane leave Rome – 10.30
- coach arrive in Berlin – 12.30
- plane arrive in New York – 3.30
- train leave London – 7.30
- plane leave San Francisco – 11.30
- train arrive in Washington – 1.30

Presentation

3a Ann will wissen, wann das Abendessen sein wird.

ANN What time will dinner be this evening?
MAN At eight instead of half past seven. There will be an announcement in 15 minutes, at quarter past ten. The next announcement will be at quarter to eleven.

Zusatzwortschatz

breakfast	Frühstück
lunch	Mittagessen
tea	Teezeit

Practice

3b Üben Sie jetzt die Viertelstunden.

A When will *(breakfast)* be, please?
B At quarter *(past seven)*. And the coach will leave an hour later.
A At quarter *(past eight)*?
B Yes, that's right.

breakfast – 7.15 • lunch – 1.15 • coffee – 3.15 • dinner – 7.15 • breakfast – 7.45 • lunch – 12.45 • tea – 3.45 • dinner – 6.45

half past seven
(*halb acht*)

half past eight
(*halb neun*)

4 Hören Sie nun den gesamten Dialog.

Information & Tips

„halb eins" – „drei viertel eins"

Oft sind Engländer und Deutsche eine Stunde zu spät oder eine Stunde zu früh zu einer Verabredung gekommen, weil sie die Uhrzeiten durcheinander gebracht haben. Beispielsweise heißt „halb eins" (12.30 Uhr) im Englischen half past twelve, nicht half past one. Half past one ist „halb zwei" (13.30 Uhr). Für „drei viertel eins" gibt es im Englischen keine direkte Entsprechung. Für „Viertel vor eins" und „drei viertel eins" gibt es nur den einen Ausdruck (a) quarter to one.

am und pm

Der Tag hat natürlich auch in Großbritannien und den USA 24 Stunden, für die Zeitangabe werden aber – außer in Fahrplänen usw. – nur die Ziffern 1 bis 12 gebraucht. „Wir werden uns um 19.00 Uhr treffen" heißt dann We will meet at 7 o'clock. Nun kann zwar 7 o'clock auch „sieben Uhr morgens" sein, aber normalerweise wird aus dem Situationszusammenhang klar, ob morgens oder abends gemeint ist. Man kann in the morning / in the afternoon / in the evening hinzufügen, um Missverständnisse zu vermeiden.
In Prospekten, Zeitungen und anderen schriftlichen Texten findet man mit Zeitangaben die Abkürzungen am und pm, also beispielsweise 7 am und 7 pm. In einer Hotelinformation könnte z. B. stehen, dass das Frühstück um 7.30 am und das Abendessen um 7.30 pm serviert wird. Das Frühstück wird natürlich morgens und das Abendessen abends gegessen. Es ist also klar, was es mit den beiden Abkürzungen auf sich hat. Beide kommen aus dem Lateinischen. Die Abkürzung am steht für ante meridiem und bedeutet „vor Mittag"; pm steht für post meridiem und bedeutet „nach Mittag".

! Zusammen mit o'clock können am und pm nicht verwendet werden: At 6 o'clock am ist also falsch. Richtig muss es at six o'clock oder at six am heißen.

Grammar

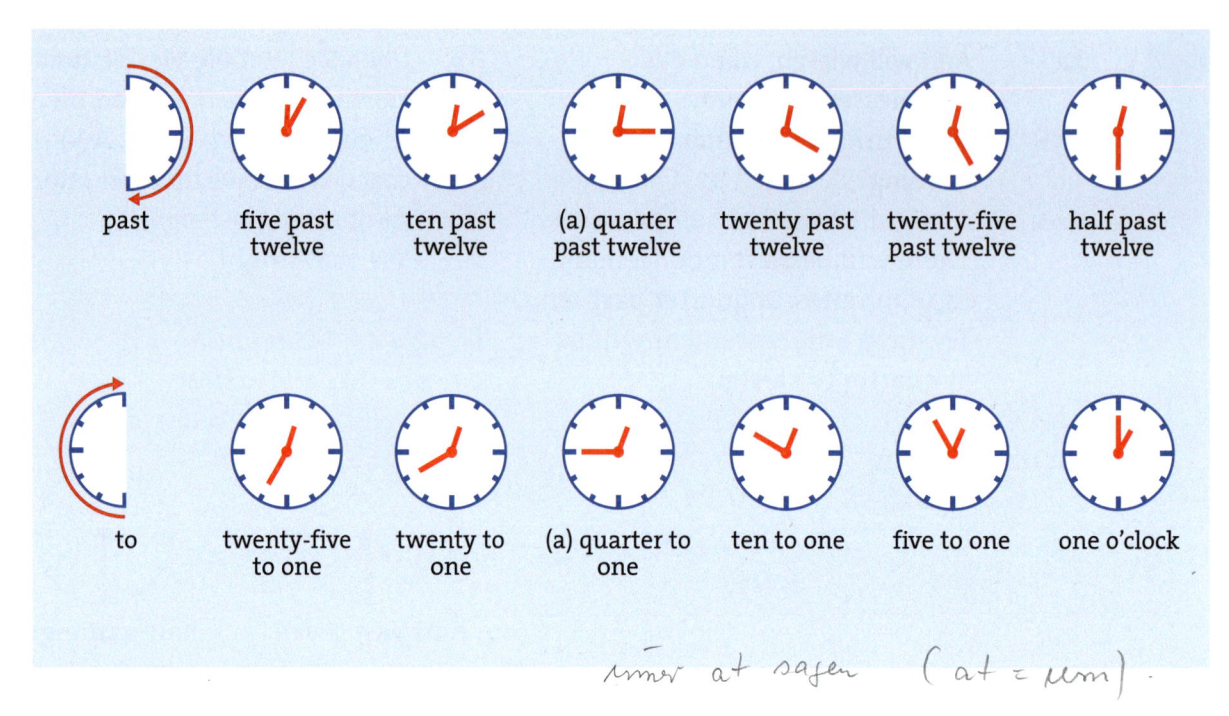

| past | five past twelve | ten past twelve | (a) quarter past twelve | twenty past twelve | twenty-five past twelve | half past twelve |

| to | twenty-five to one | twenty to one | (a) quarter to one | ten to one | five to one | one o'clock |

immer at sagen (at = um).

When **will** I/we see you?
He/She **will** arrive at 6 o'clock.
There **will** be an announcement at 5.30.
You/They **will** meet Ann later.

💡 **will** ist für alle Personen gleich.
Es bedeutet „werden".
Mit **will** sprechen wir über die Zukunft.

Useful Phrases

Track 59

What time is it? / What is the time? — Wie spät ist es?
What time / When will dinner be? — Um wie viel Uhr / Wann wird das Abendessen sein?
Dinner is at 8 o'clock. — Das Abendessen ist um 8.00 Uhr.
Lunch is in one hour / in ten minutes. — Das Mittagessen ist in einer Stunde / in zehn Minuten.
How much time will we have in Tangier? — Wie viel Zeit werden wir in Tanger haben?

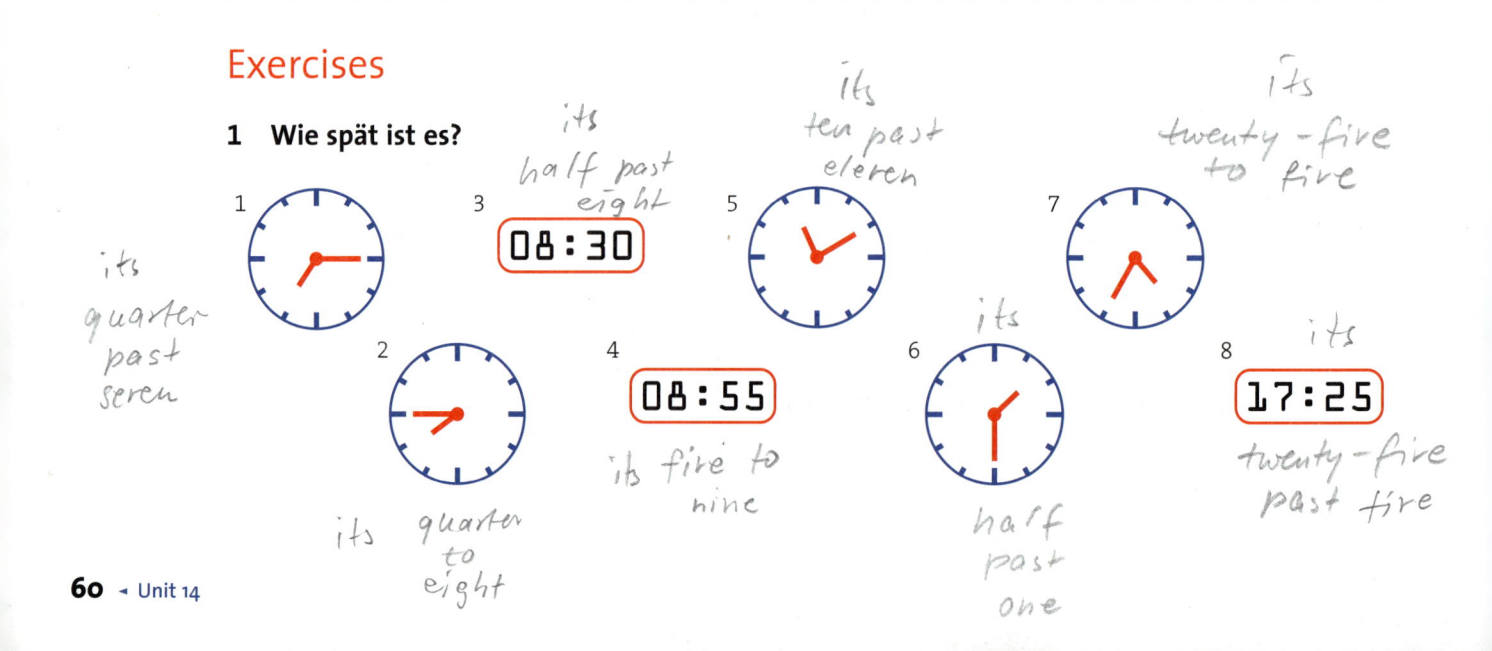

Exercises

1 Wie spät ist es?

1. *its quarter past seven*
2. *its quarter to eight*
3. *its half past eight* — 08:30
4. *its five to nine* — 08:55
5. *its ten past eleven*
6. *its half past one*
7. *its twenty-five to five*
8. *its twenty-five past five* — 17:25

Unit 14

Exercises

2 Schreiben Sie die passenden Fragen mit When will …? und What time will …?

> Breakfast will be at 7.45 am, and the coach to Oxford will leave at 8.30 am.
> We will arrive there at 10 am. You will have time to visit some of the colleges.
> We will meet again at 1 pm. Lunch will be at 1.30 pm in a nice old Oxford pub.

Annotations: vormittags, morgens / Reisebus / Institut / Mittagessen / nachmittags, abend

1. _When will_ breakfast _be_ ? – At 7.45.
2. What time _will_ the coach to Oxford _leave_ ? – At 8.30.
3. When _will_ we _arrive_ there? – At 10 am.
4. What time _will_ we _meet_ again? – At 1 pm.
5. When _will_ lunch _be_ ? – At 1.30 pm.

3a Ergänzen Sie passende Zeiten.

In my house …
- breakfast is at _seven o'clock_ (or _half past seven_).
- lunch is at _twelve o'clock_ (or _half past twelve_).
- dinner is at _seven o'clock_ (or _half past seven_).

3b Und nun fragen Sie sich gegenseitig: What time … / When is … in your house?

4 Bringen Sie die Begriffe in eine logische Reihenfolge.

1. breakfast, dinner, lunch, tea — _breakfast, lunch, tea, dinner_
2. half past two, twenty-five to three, twenty-five past two, half past three
   (14.30, 14.35, 14:25, 15:30)
   twenty-five past two, half past two, twenty-five to three, half past three
3. very beautiful, lovely, awful, OK — _awful, OK, lovely, very beautiful_
   (schrecklich)

5 Wissen Sie noch, wie es heißt?

1. Entschuldigen Sie. Wie spät ist es?
   Excuse my, what time is it?
2. Wann wird das Schiff wieder abfahren? – Um halb acht.
   When will the ship leave again? At half past seven
3. Also wie viel Zeit werden wir dort haben? – Achteinhalb Stunden.
   So how much time will we have there?
   Eight and a half hours.
4. Um wie viel Uhr wird das Abendessen heute Abend sein?
   What time will dinner be this evening?

Unit 14 ▶ 61

15 Revision

Wortschatz:

a Arbeiten Sie zusammen mit einem anderen Kursmitglied. Ergänzen Sie die Tabelle mit jeweils zwei passenden Begriffen.

Verkehrsmittel	Mahlzeiten	Tiere	Kinder	Gebäude
coach	lunch	animal	children	museum
train	dinner	cat	boy	theatre
plane	breakfast	dog	girl	church

Wortschatz:

b Ordnen Sie mit Ihrem Partner / Ihrer Partnerin die Begriffe den Zeichnungen zu.

shop • cinema • theatre • river • swimming pool • church • castle • pub • night club • restaurant • sports centre

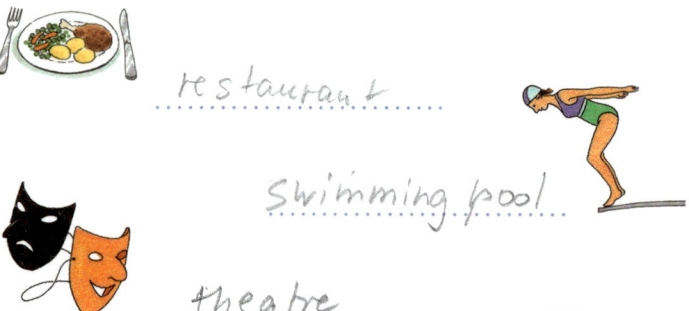

restaurant
pub 
swimming pool
theatre
cinema 
shop 
church 
night club 
castle 
river 
sport centre 

Redewendungen: Einladungen

a Erfinden Sie mit Ihrem Partner / Ihrer Partnerin einen neuen Wohnort.
Wählen Sie aus Übung **b** oben sechs Gebäude/Einrichtungen, die es in Ihrer Fantasiestadt gibt. Schreiben Sie sie auf.

b Eine/r aus jedem Paar (der Gast) „besucht" (mit der Liste) ein anderes Paar (Gastgeber/in) und fragt nach den Gebäuden/Einrichtungen auf deren Liste.

GAST	Is there a *(swimming pool)* here?
GASTGEBER/IN	Yes, there is. / No, there isn't.
GAST	*(Tell me about it, please.)*
GASTGEBER/IN	*(Well, it's very modern.)*

Grammatik:
Ordnen Sie den Ziffern den richtigen Buchstaben zu.

1. I have a son. — **D**
2. Is there an Italian restaurant near here? — **A**
3. Can I have some water, please? — **E**
4. Are there any nice pubs here? — **F**
5. Are there any Americans here? — **B**
6. When will the coach leave? — **C**

A. Yes, there is. Da Mario in Market Street.
B. Yes, there are. Jack and Kate Warner from Chicago.
C. At about 7 o'clock.
D. He's married and has two children.
E. Yes, of course. Here you are.
F. No, there aren't, I'm afraid. But there's one in the next village.

Die Uhrzeit
Bilden Sie zwei Gruppen.

Gruppe A beginnt. Ein Kursmitglied nennt eine Uhrzeit (nur volle Stunden!). Ein zweites gibt eine Minutenzahl zwischen 5 und 55 an (nur in 5er Schritten!). Ein drittes ernennt eine Person aus Gruppe B. Dieses Kursmitglied muss die neue Uhrzeit sagen. Wenn die Uhrzeit richtig gesagt wird, ist Gruppe B dran.

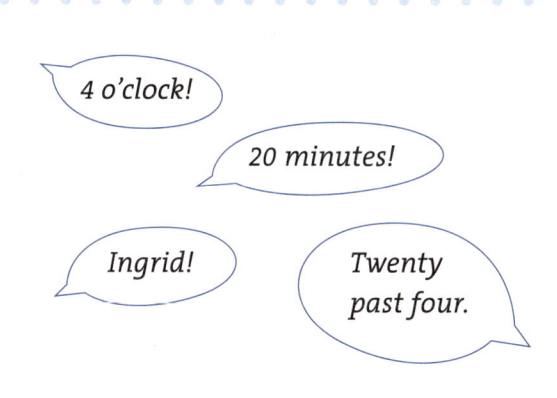

4 o'clock!
20 minutes!
Ingrid!
Twenty past four.

Rückblick
In Units 11–14 haben Sie unter anderem gelernt, wie man …

… jemanden über seinen Wohnort befragt.	Tell me about *(Oxford)*. What is there to do and see? – There's …
… jemanden fragt, ob er Lust hat, etwas Bestimmtes zu machen.	Would you like to *(see some photos)*?
… darauf antwortet.	Yes, please. / No, thank you. Later perhaps.
… über seine Familie/Freunde erzählt.	I have a *(daughter)*. *(She has two children.)*
… nach der Uhrzeit fragt.	What time is it, please? – It's *(half past six)*.

16 It's lovely to get up late!

Presentation

1a Ann und Inge erzählen von ihrem Tag.

ANN It's lovely to get up late! I usually get up at seven o'clock. What about you?

INGE I usually get up at six. I start work at half past seven.

ANN That's early.

Zusatzwortschatz

have breakfast	frühstücken	finish work	aufhören zu arbeiten
have lunch	zu Mittag essen	go to bed	ins Bett gehen
have dinner/supper	zu Abend essen		

Practice

1b Berichten Sie von Ihrem Tagesablauf.

A I usually *(get up)* at … What about you?
B I usually *(get up)* at …

get up • have breakfast • start work • have lunch • finish work • have dinner • go to bed

---

2a Inge erzählt, dass sie Teilzeit arbeitet.

INGE I work on Monday, Tuesday and Thursday.
ANN Oh, you work part-time.
INGE Yes, that's right. What about you?
ANN I work full-time.

2b Sind Sie berufstätig?

A *(I'm retired.)* What about you?
B *(I work part-time.)*
(I work full-time. / I'm a housewife.)

2c Berichten Sie von Ihrem Samstag.

A On Saturday I usually *(get up)* at … What about you?
B On Saturday I usually *(get up)* at …

get up • have breakfast • have lunch • have supper • go to bed

Zusatzwortschatz

Wednesday	Mittwoch	Sunday	Sonntag
Friday	Freitag	I'm a housewife.	Ich bin Hausfrau.
Saturday	Samstag	I'm retired.	Ich bin im Ruhestand.

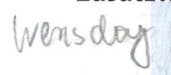

Presentation

3a Ann und Inge erzählen, was sie in ihrer Freizeit machen.

INGE What about your free time?
ANN Well, in the evening I often watch TV or read. But on Tuesday I always go to a gymnastics class.
INGE And I always go to my English class.
ANN On Tuesday?
INGE Yes, and on Thursday I often meet friends.
ANN I sometimes have lunch with friends on Sunday.

Zusatzwortschatz

never	nie
I listen to music/the radio.	Ich höre Musik/Radio.
I work in the garden.	Ich arbeite im Garten.

Practice

3b Erzählen Sie, was Sie in Ihrer Freizeit machen.

A What about your free time?
B In the evening I …
   On *(Saturday)* I …
   (I sometimes/often/usually/always …)

work in the garden • go to my … club/class • visit/meet … • go for a drink/meal • have lunch/dinner with … • go to the cinema/theatre • go shopping • watch TV/read • listen to music/the radio

4 Hören Sie nun den gesamten Dialog.

Information & Tips

Berufsangaben

Für Berufe wie „Lehrer/in" (teacher), „Arzt/Ärztin" (doctor), „Verkäufer/in" (shop assistant) und viele andere Berufe gibt es im Englischen eine direkte Entsprechung. Manche deutsche Berufsbezeichnungen, z. B. „Sachbearbeiter/in" oder „kaufmännische/r Angestellte/r", sind aber schwer ins Englische zu übertragen. Es wird also nicht immer leicht sein, für Ihren Beruf bzw. die Berufe Ihrer Kinder oder Enkelkinder eine englische Entsprechung zu finden.

! Im Englischen wird a/an mit Berufsbezeichnungen gebraucht z. B.:
My daughter is a teacher
(Meine Tochter ist Lehrerin).

Arbeitszeiten

In Großbritannien beginnt der Arbeitstag in der Regel später als bei uns. Er beginnt normalerweise gegen neun und endet gegen fünf Uhr.
Insgesamt ist der Tagesablauf in Großbritannien etwas nach hinten verschoben. Schulen beginnen um 9.00, nicht um 8.00 Uhr. Die Mahlzeiten werden meistens entsprechend später als bei uns eingenommen. Übrigens: Für eine Mahlzeit, das Abendessen, gibt es im Englischen zwei Wörter, supper und dinner. Supper bezeichnet ein leichteres oder alltägliches Abendessen. Dinner (wie in dem Fernsehsketch Dinner for One) ist die Bezeichnung für ein umfangreicheres oder festliches Abendessen.

Grammar

I get up at six.
I work part-time.

I **always/never** get up late.
Ich stehe immer/nie spät auf.
I **usually/often/sometimes** get up late.
Ich stehe gewöhnlich/oft/manchmal spät auf.

I go to a gymnastics class **on Tuesday**.
On Tuesday I go to a gymnastics class.
I watch TV **in the evening**.
In the evening I watch TV.
I have supper **at six o'clock**.
At six o'clock I have supper.

- Aussagen über Dinge, die wir regelmäßig tun, werden wie im Deutschen gemacht.

- always und never stehen immer direkt vor dem Verb. Auch usually, often und sometimes stehen meist vor dem Verb; sie können aber auch am Satzanfang oder -ende stehen. Keines dieser Wörter kann, wie im Deutschen, hinter dem Verb stehen.

- Zeitangaben mit Wochentagen (z. B. on Tuesday), mit Tageszeiten (z. B. in the evening) und mit Uhrzeiten (z. B. at six o'clock) stehen am Satzanfang oder Satzende.

Useful Phrases

Track 64

It's lovely to get up late.	*Es ist schön, spät aufzustehen.*
I start work at eight o'clock.	*Ich fange um acht Uhr an zu arbeiten.*
I finish work at four o'clock.	*Ich höre um vier Uhr auf zu arbeiten.*
I'm retired / a housewife.	*Ich bin im Ruhestand/Hausfrau.*
I work full-time / part-time.	*Ich arbeite Vollzeit/Teilzeit.*
I go to an English class.	*Ich besuche einen Englischkurs.*
What about you?	*Was ist mit Ihnen? / Wie ist es mit Ihnen?*

Exercises

1 Ergänzen Sie den Text zu Anns Tagesablauf mit den Ausdrücken im Kasten.

leave the house • work • read • get up • finish work • start work • watch TV • have supper • have breakfast • go shopping • go • have lunch

I *get up* at seven o'clock. Then I *have breakfast* – cornflakes, toast and tea. I *leave the house* at half past eight and *start work* at nine. I *work* full-time. I *have lunch* at one o'clock in our canteen, and I *finish work* at half past four. I often *go shopping* – there's a shop near my house. I *have supper* at six or half past six – it's usually a hot meal. In the evening I *watch TV* or I *read*. But on Tuesday I *go* to a gymnastics class.

Exercises

2 Kreuzworträtsel

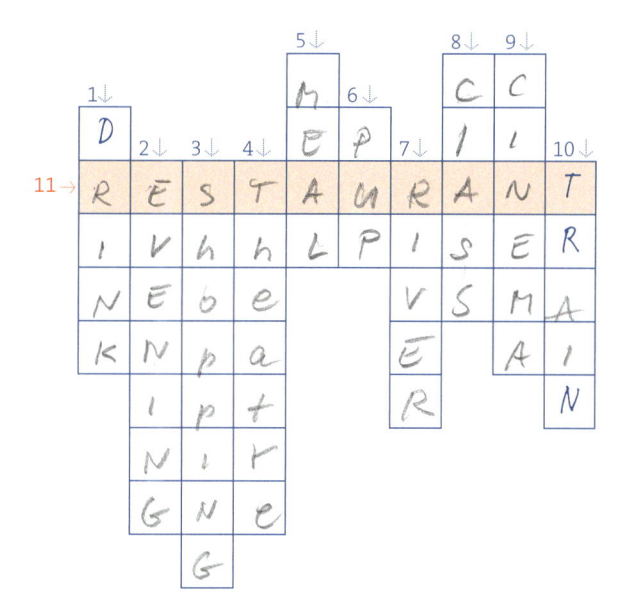

11 → RESTAURANT

1. go for a d r i n k (wine, beer, juice, ...)
2. go to the Sterling Silver e v e n i n g class
3. go s h o p p i n g (in Aldi, in Kaufhof, in ...)
4. go to the t h e a t r e (and see Goethe, Schiller, Shakespeare, ...)
5. go for a m e a l (pizza, steak & salad, ...)
6. go to the p u b (and meet friends for a beer)
7. go on the r i v e r (in a boat)
8. go to a (gymnastics) c l a s s
9. go to the C I N E M A (and see a film)
10. go on a tr a i n (to Oxford, London, ...)

11 RESTAURANT

3a Setzen Sie das Wort an die Stelle, an der es normalerweise steht. Manchmal gibt es mehr als eine richtige Lösung.

1. I listen to the radio. (sometimes) _I sometimes listen to the radio._
2. I have coffee and toast. (in the morning) _(or) in the morning I have ---_
3. I have lunch in town. (always) _I always have ---_
4. I go to my choir. (on Friday) _(or) on Friday ---_
5. I finish work. (at four o'clock) _(or) At four o'clock I finish work_
6. I go to bed late. (usually) _I usually go to ---_
7. I watch TV. (often) _I often watch ---_
8. I get up early. (never) _I never get up early_

3b Und jetzt wählen Sie drei Sätze aus. Ändern Sie die Zeitangabe so, dass der Satz für Sie passt.

Beispiel (Satz 3): *I never have lunch in town. I always have lunch at home.*

17 I don't often eat a big breakfast

Presentation

1a Ann freut sich, dass sie viel Zeit im Urlaub hat.

ANN I don't often eat a big breakfast. I don't usually have time when I'm at home! What about you?

INGE I don't have a big lunch. But I always have a good breakfast. I start work at half past seven. But I always have time.

ANN You get up at six, right?

INGE Yes. It's how I always start the day. Up at six, twenty minutes for breakfast, with some nice hot coffee, bread, cheese and sausage – and then I go to work.

Practice

1b Erzählen Sie, was Sie gewöhnlich nicht machen.

A I don't *(usually/often)* … What about you?

B I …

get up early / late on Sunday • have a big breakfast / lunch / supper • go to bed early/late • visit my sister/brother • read/listen to the radio in bed • go to the theatre/cinema • go shopping on Monday • watch TV in the morning

Presentation

Track 66

2a **Ann beschreibt das englische Frühstück.**

ANN In Britain we don't usually eat cheese and sausage for breakfast.
INGE And people don't drink coffee, only tea. Is that right?
ANN Well, some people have tea, some have coffee. But it's often instant coffee.

Zusatzwortschatz

roll	Brötchen	fruit	Obst	muesli	Müsli
jam	Marmelade	ham	Schinken	fish	Fisch
cornflakes	Cornflakes	bacon and eggs	Schinkenspeck und Eier		

Practice

2b **Erzählen Sie, was Sie frühstücken.**

A I usually have … for breakfast. What about you?
B I have / don't have …

2c **Sagen Sie, was man bei uns normalerweise nicht zum Frühstück isst und trinkt.**

| We They People | don't | usually often | eat drink have | … |

Track 67

3a **Und das Abendessen?**

INGE What about supper?
ANN Well, supper is often a hot meal.
INGE You mean people don't have bread and cheese and sausage?
ANN Not usually.
INGE That's our normal supper. And Bruno has a bottle of beer.
ANN People don't usually drink beer with their supper in Britain. I don't like beer much. But I like wine.

3b **Sagen Sie, welche der genannten Speisen und Getränke Sie mögen, welche nicht.**

A I like *(beer)*. / I don't like *(beer)* much. What about you?
B …

Track 68

4 **Hören Sie nun den gesamten Dialog.**

Information & Tips

breakfast

Das traditionelle englische Frühstück besteht aus: Müsli oder Cornflakes, Schinkenspeck und Eiern, Toast und Butter mit Orangenmarmelade. Heutzutage werden Schinkenspeck und Eier nicht mehr so häufig gegessen.

Übrigens: Zum Toast und zur (meist gesalzenen) Butter gibt es marmalade. Marmalade ist immer aus Zitrusfrüchten hergestellt (Orangen, Zitronen, Grapefruit); andere Konfitüren heißen jam.

Grammar

I'm German. **I'm not** Austrian.
You're young. **You aren't** old.
We're early. **We aren't** late.
They're new. **They aren't** old.

I like wine. I **don't** like beer.
You work part-time. You **don't** work full-time.
We read. We **don't** watch TV.
They speak English. They **don't** speak French.

I **often** drink tea for breakfast.
I don't **often** drink coffee.

- am und are, d. h die Teile des Verbs be, werden verneint, indem man das Wort not dahinter setzt oder die Kurzform n't anhängt.

- Verben außer be werden verneint, indem man das Wort don't vor das Verb stellt. don't ist die Kurzform von do not.

- Zeitbestimmungen wie always, usually, often, sometimes stehen vor dem Hauptverb, d. h. in verneinten Sätzen hinter don't.

seldom – selten

Useful Phrases

Track 69

I don't have a big breakfast.	Ich frühstücke nicht viel.
I don't have a big lunch/supper.	Ich esse nicht viel zu Mittag/Abend.
I don't have time.	Ich habe keine Zeit.
Not usually.	Gewöhnlich nicht.
I like wine.	Ich mag/trinke gern Wein.
I don't like beer.	Ich mag kein Bier.

Exercises

1 Ergänzen Sie den Text über Anns Wochenende mit don't und den Ausdrücken im Kasten.

get up • go • go to • go shopping • have • like • visit • ~~work~~

I don't work on Saturday, so I *don't get up* [also] very early. I have a late breakfast, but I *don't have* a big breakfast – only [nur] cornflakes, toast and tea. I *don't go shopping* on Saturday morning – the shops are always [immer] full. I usually go in the afternoon [nachmittag]. I *don't go to* the theatre very often, but I sometimes go on Saturday evening. On Sunday I sometimes visit friends, or they visit me. I *don't visit* my relatives very often – they're too far from Oxford. Well, I have a cousin in London, that's not very far, but I *don't like* his wife very much so I *don't go* [also] there very often.

Exercises

2 Trifft Folgendes auch auf Sie zu?
Bejahen Sie mit I …, too oder verneinen Sie mit I don't …

1 ANN: I live in Oxford. *I don't live in Oxford*
2 BRUNO: I like red wine. *I like red wine, too*
3 INGE: I eat a big breakfast. *I eat a big breakfast, too*
4 ANN: I eat a hot meal in the evening. *I don't eat a hot meal in the evening*
5 BRUNO: I drink beer with my evening meal. *I don't drink beer with my evening meal*
6 INGE: I often go to bed late. *I don't often go to bed late*
7 ANN: I work full-time. *I don't work full-time*
8 INGE: I go to my English class on Tuesday. *I don't go to my English class on Tuesday*
9 BRUNO: I get up late on Sunday. *I don't get up late on Sunday*

3 Kann das Wort an der mit • gekennzeichneten Stelle stehen?

			Yes	No
1	often	We • have lunch with friends on Sunday.	X	
2	often	We don't visit • our relatives.		X
3	usually	I don't get up • early.		X
4	usually	In the evening I • watch TV.	X	
5	sometimes	I • have an egg for breakfast.	X	
6	sometimes	We have • a bottle of wine in the evening.		X
7	always	• I go shopping on Friday.		X
8	always	We don't • go to Spain.	X	

4 Ordnen Sie zu.

> You can have …
> a cold lunch • ~~instant coffee~~ • some fruit juice • cold milk • a bottle of wine •
> a hot meal • ~~an egg~~ • some sausages *(österreichisch)*
> *Würstchen*

You can eat …
an egg
a cold lunch
a hot meal
some sausage (österr.)

You can drink …
instant coffee
some fruit juice
cold milk
a bottle of wine

Wurst = cold meat

18 Tell me about your son

Presentation

1a Track 70

Inge fragt nach Anns Sohn.

INGE   Tell me about your son.
ANN   Well, he lives in Ebersberg and works in Munich. He works a lot. But at the weekend he does a lot of sport. In the summer he goes windsurfing on the Chiemsee. In the autumn he goes hiking in the mountains. And in the winter and in the spring he goes skiing. His wife likes music. She sings in a choir. They sometimes go to concerts in Munich.
INGE   Bavaria is a nice place to live.

Practice

1b Was wissen Sie von den anderen Kursmitgliedern?
(Ingrid gets up late on Sunday.)
(Alfons works full-time.)
(Karin's son lives in Berlin.)

get up • work • live • read • meet • like • eat • drink • sing • visit • watch • listen to • do sport • go hiking • go skiing • go shopping • come to the English class • go to the theatre

Presentation

2a **Inge erzählt von einem typischen Sonntag.**

Track 71

ANN And Euskirchen?

INGE Well, you can go hiking, or sometimes skiing in the Eifel. But Euskirchen isn't Munich.

ANN What is a typical Sunday for you?

INGE Well, in the winter Sunday is quiet. I get up late and have breakfast with Bruno. Then I read the weekend newspaper. I go to church. Then I cook lunch and sometimes make a cake. After lunch I often go for a walk with Bruno and the dog. Then I phone or write a letter or an email to my daughter. In the evening we often watch TV. But in the summer it's different.

Practice

2b **Sagen sie, was Inge am Sonntag macht.**

A She gets up late and …

2c **Jetzt fragen Sie Ihre Nachbarin / Ihren Nachbarn.**

A What is a typical Sunday for you?

B I …

2d **Nun berichten Sie der Klasse, was Ihr/e Nachbar/in gesagt hat.**

A *(Ingrid gets up early …)*

3 **Hören Sie nun den gesamten Dialog.**

Track 72

Information & Tips

Sonntag

Sonntag ist in den englischsprachigen Ländern nicht so ein ruhiger Tag wie bei uns. In Großbritannien z. B. haben etliche Geschäfte geöffnet und man kann einkaufen gehen. In den Wohnsiedlungen werden Autos vor dem Haus gewaschen; im Sommer knattern die Rasenmäher in den Gärten.

Zur festen Sonntagsroutine gehört für manche Briten das Zeitunglesen. Die Zeitungsverlage drucken am Sonntag besonders dicke Ausgaben (zusätzlich zu den Ausgaben, die am Samstag erscheinen). Zum Sonntag gehört natürlich auch – allerdings für einen immer kleiner werdenden Bevölkerungsteil – der Kirchgang.

Die meisten Gläubigen sind Mitglieder in der anglikanischen Staatskirche. Die Riten der anglikanischen Kirche ähneln denen der katholischen Kirche. Die Glaubensrichtung ist aber protestantisch. Neben den westlich orientierten Glaubensgemeinschaften gibt es aber auch eine beträchtliche Anzahl von Moslems. In den USA, wo noch ein recht hoher Bevölkerungsanteil regelmäßig zur Kirche geht, gibt es eine Vielzahl unterschiedlichster Glaubensgemeinschaften.

! „in die Kirche gehen" heißt auf Englisch go to church (nicht go to the church). Ähnlich sind die Ausdrücke go to bed und go to school (in die Schule gehen).

Grammar

I work part-time.	He/She works full-time.
You live in Germany.	He/She lives in England.
We like music.	He/She likes music, too.

I go	he/she goes
I do	he/she does
I finish	he/she finishes
I watch	he/she watches

have – has (handwritten)

In the summer we go to Spain.
She goes hiking in the autumn.
At the weekend I get up late.

- 💡 he, she, it – das „s" muss mit!

- 💡 Den Verben go und do sowie allen Verben, die auf -s, -sh oder -ch enden, wird -es statt -s angehängt.

- 💡 Zeitbestimmungen wie in the summer und at the weekend stehen am Satzanfang oder Satzende.

Useful Phrases

Track 73

Tell me about your son.	Erzählen Sie mir von Ihrem Sohn.
Bavaria is a nice place to live.	In Bayern kann man gut leben.
After lunch I go for a walk.	Nach dem Mittagessen gehe ich spazieren.
I write an email / a letter to my daughter.	Ich schreibe eine E-Mail / einen Brief an meine Tochter.
In the summer it's different.	Im Sommer ist es anders.

Exercises

1 Ergänzen Sie die Sätze unten mithilfe der Angaben ohne Verneinungen einzusetzen.

	ANN'S SON	INGE'S DAUGHTER
live	Germany	United States
work	Munich	Boston
go hiking	yes	–
go to concerts	yes	yes
cook	yes	–
watch TV	–	yes

Ann's son _lives_ in Germany. He _works_ in Munich.
In his free time he _goes hiking_ and he _goes to concerts_.
He _cooks_, too. His wife likes that.
Inge's daughter _lives_ in the United States. She _works_ in Boston. In her free time she _goes to concert_ and _she watches TV_.

Exercises

2 Berichten Sie, was in der Sprechblase steht.

I get up at 7.00. Then I have breakfast. I leave the house at 8.30 (half past eight) and start work at 9.00. I work full-time. I finish work at 4.30 (half past four).

She gets up at 7.00. Then she has breakfast. She leaves the house at 8.30 and starts work at 9.00. She works full-time. She finishes work at 4.30

Wissen Sie noch, von welcher Person die Rede ist? Ann

3 a Sagen Sie, was Bruno macht, was Inge macht und was beide machen.

Verwenden Sie: **He … / She … / They both …**

	BRUNO	INGE
play (plays)	cards	tennis
like (likes)	wine	wine
go (goes)	to the pub	hiking
	to a cookery class (*Kochkurs*)	to an English class
meet (meets)	his bowling club friends	friends on the internet
speak (speaks)	German & English	German & English

3 b Schreiben Sie auf (einen gesonderten Zettel), was aus der Tabelle auf Sie zutrifft.

Beispiele: *I play cards. / I like red wine. / I go hiking.*

3 c Tauschen Sie Zettel mit einem anderen Kursmitglied. Erzählen Sie der Klasse, welche Gemeinsamkeiten es zwischen Ihnen und dem anderen Kursmitglied gibt.

Beispiel: *I play cards and (Ingrid) plays cards, too. We both play cards.*

4 Was ist richtig? Streichen Sie das Falsche durch.

1 She writes a letter *at/to* her son.
2 We go shopping *after lunch / after the lunch*.
3 *At/On* Monday I go to my English class.
4 She goes skiing *on/in* the winter.
5 They go *to bed / to the bed* late.
6 Inge goes *in/to* church on Sunday.
7 *In/At* the afternoon I sometimes make a cake.
8 We sometimes *make/go* for a walk.

5 Wissen Sie noch, wie es heißt?

1 Am Wochenende treibt er viel Sport. At the weekend he does a lot of sport
2 Seine Frau mag Musik. His wife likes musik
3 Dann lese ich manchmal die Zeitung. Then sometimes I read the newspaper
4 In Bayern kann man gut leben. Bavaria is a nice place to live

One can live well in Bavaria (man)

19 What's the weather like in Madeira?

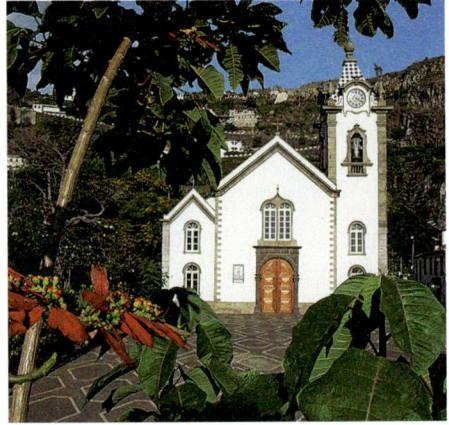

wie is das Wetter in Madeira

Presentation

1a **Das Schiff legt morgen in Madeira an.**

ANN The ship stops in Madeira tomorrow.
INGE Yes. It's a lovely place. *— schön, herrlich*
ANN Oh, you know it?
INGE Yes. Every year in the winter we have a holiday in the sun. Bruno doesn't like the winter. He doesn't like the cold. He likes the summer best. *am besten / liebsten*
ANN I don't mind the cold. But I don't like the heat. *Ich kümmere mich nicht um die Kälte / mir macht die Kälte nichts aus*

Practice

1b **Erzählen Sie Ihrer Nachbarin / Ihrem Nachbarn, was Sie (nicht) mögen.**

A I like / don't like the autumn/winter.
I like the … best.
I don't like / don't mind the heat/cold.
I usually have / don't usually have a holiday in the spring/…

1c **Die Klasse versucht zu raten, was einzelne Kursteilnehmer gesagt haben.**

C (Ingrid doesn't like the winter.)
D (She likes the summer best.)
E (She doesn't like the cold.)
F (She doesn't usually have a holiday in the summer.)

Nun berichtet der/die Nachbar/in, was der/die Kursteilnehmer/in wirklich gesagt hat.

B (Ingrid …)

Presentation

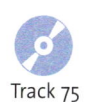

2a **Inge erzählt über Madeiras Klima.**
Track 75
ANN   What's the climate like in Madeira?
INGE   It doesn't get too hot. It doesn't get too cold. It doesn't snow.
(Es ist nicht zu kalt)
ANN   What about rain?
INGE   It rains. But it doesn't rain too much. It's nice and warm.

Practice

2b **Wie ist das Klima woanders?**
A   What's the climate like *(in Texas)*?
B   In the spring/summer/autumn/winter it …

… rains/doesn't rain	(a lot).	
… snows/doesn't snow		
… gets	(very)	hot.
… doesn't get	(too)	cold.

in Texas • in Alaska • in London • in Rome • in Mallorca • in north Germany • in south Germany • where we live

3a **Ann und Inge planen ihren Landgang.** *(sollen)*
Track 76
ANN   What shall we do in Funchal?
INGE   Well, there's a very nice market. Shall we go there?
ANN   Yes, that's a nice idea. — *Idee*
INGE   And shall we visit the cathedral?
(lieber nicht) ANN   I'd rather not. *würde*
INGE   OK, let's go to the market.
ANN   We can buy some souvenirs.
INGE   Bruno wants to buy some Madeira wine. *wollen*

3b **A macht Vorschläge.**
B nimmt sie an oder lehnt sie ab.
A   Shall we *(go to the market)* now? *(sollen)*
B   That's a nice idea. Let's do that. / I'd rather not. *würde*

go to the market • go shopping • go to a jazz concert • have some tea • go for a drink • go for an Italian meal • go to the cinema • watch TV

4 **Hören Sie nun den gesamten Dialog.**
Track 77

Information & Tips

Das Wetter

Das Wetter in Großbritannien ist besser als sein Ruf. Das Klima ist wegen des Golfstroms vor der Westküste milder als bei uns. In Torquay in Südwestengland gibt es sogar Palmen und subtropische Pflanzen. Dass man Winterreifen auf sein Auto aufzieht, ist fast unbekannt. Und viele unterscheiden bei ihrer Kleidung nicht zwischen Sommer- und Winterschuhen.

In Schottland ist das allerdings anders – dort kann man auch Wintersport treiben.

What's the weather like?

Das Wort like in Fragen wie What's the climate like? hat nichts mit dem Verb like (mögen) zu tun. What's … like? ist eine Frage nach der Art oder Beschaffenheit von etwas und bedeutet „Wie ist …?"

Grammar

I like the summer.	I **don't** like the winter.
Bruno likes the summer.	He **doesn't** like the winter.
Ann wants to buy souvenirs.	She **doesn't** want to go to the cathedral.
It rains.	But it **doesn't** rain much.

💡 In Unit 17 haben Sie bereits gelernt, dass Verben (außer be) verneint werden, indem man das Wort don't (do not) davor stellt.

💡 In der dritten Person (nach he, she, it) wird doesn't (does not) statt don't vor das Verb gesetzt.

Useful Phrases

Track 78

What's the weather like?	*Wie ist das Wetter?*
He likes the summer best.	*Er mag den Sommer am liebsten.*
I don't mind the cold.	*Mir macht die Kälte nichts aus.*
It's nice and warm.	*Es ist schön warm.*
Shall we go to the cathedral?	*Sollen wir zur Kathedrale gehen?*
Let's go to the market.	*Lassen Sie uns / Lasst uns zum Markt gehen.*
I'd rather not.	*Lieber nicht.*

Exercises

1 Ergänzen Sie den Text unten mit Verb + s oder doesn't + Verb.

	CHRIS	MONIKA
work	full-time	part-time
speak	English, German	German, English, Italian
sing in choir	no	yes
do sport	yes	no
go to church	no	yes
like	spring, summer	spring, autumn

Chris and Monika live in Bavaria. Chris _works_ full-time, but Monika _doesn't work_ full-time. She only _works_ part-time. Chris _speaks_ German and Monika _speaks_ English. She also _speaks_ Italian, but Chris _doesn't speak_ Italian. In her free time Monika _sings_ in a choir. Chris _doesn't sing_ in a choir, but he _does_ a lot of sport. On Sunday Monika _goes_ to church. But Chris _doesn't go_ to church. Chris _likes_ the spring and the summer best. Monika _doesn't like_ the summer – she _likes_ the autumn. But she _likes_ the spring, too. They both like the spring.

Exercises

2 Ergänzen Sie mit der richtigen Form des Verbs in Klammern.

INGE Bruno and I (have) _have_ a holiday in the sun every winter. I (not/mind) _don't mind_ the cold, but Bruno (not/like) _doesn't like_¹ it much. We often (go) _go_ ² to Spain. We (not/have) _don't have_ ³ a holiday in the summer, but we often (go) _go_ ⁴ hiking in Bavaria in the autumn. We (want) _want_ ⁵ to visit our daughter next year. She (live) _lives_ ⁶ in the United States. She (not/come) _doesn't come_ ⁷ to Germany very often, so we (not/see) _don't see_ ⁸ our daughter a lot. She (like) _likes_ ⁹ it in the USA. She (not/want) _doesn't want_ ¹⁰ to leave.

[handwritten notes: "Ihr macht die Kälte nichts aus", "want = wollen"]

3a Schreiben Sie einen Test für ein anderes Kursmitglied.

Arbeiten Sie dabei mit einem anderen Kursmitglied zusammen. Schreiben Sie vier Sätze über Personen in der Klasse, über Orte, die Sie kennen, und das Wetter dort. Drei Ihrer Sätze sollen wahr, einer unwahr sein. Verwenden Sie, wenn Sie mögen, einige dieser Stichworte:

...	likes / doesn't like	the summer/winter/spring/autumn.
		the heat / the cold.
		hiking/sport/jazz/museums.
	drinks / doesn't drink	wine/beer/(instant) coffee/tea.
	eats / doesn't eat	a big breakfast / lunch.
		a hot evening meal.
		toast / ... .
	gets up / doesn't get up	early/late (on Sunday / ...).
	works / doesn't work	(part-time / full-time).
In ...	it rains / doesn't rain a lot.	
	it snows / doesn't snow a lot.	
	it gets / doesn't get very hot/cold (in the summer/winter).	

3b Und nun geben Sie Ihre Sätze einem anderen Paar.

Kann das andere Paar feststellen, welcher der vier Sätze unwahr ist? Diesen Satz soll das andere Paar der Klasse vorlesen und korrigieren.

4 At, in oder on?

1. _in_ the afternoon
2. _on_ Friday evening
3. _at_ six o'clock
4. _in_ the evening
5. _at_ five to two
6. _in_ one hour
7. _on_ Monday morning
8. _at_ the weekend
9. _on_ Wednesday

[handwritten notes: "At = um, am", "in = in, am", "on = am"]

20 Revision

Wochentage und Jahreszeiten

a **Ein Kursmitglied nennt einen Wochentag.**
Ein zweites sagt *Three days later* (oder gibt anstelle von *three* eine andere Zahl vor).
Ein drittes Kursmitglied nennt den neuen Wochentag.

b **Wie lauten die Jahreszeiten?**

autumn = Fall (USA)

Wortschatz: Freizeitbeschäftigungen

Ordnen Sie die Begriffe unten den Zeichnungen zu.

1 Number one is "write a letter".

- phone
- work in the garden
- listen to music
- make a cake
- go shopping
- ~~write a letter~~
- go skiing
- go to the theatre
- go for a walk
- read the newspaper
- meet friends
- cook
- go to a restaurant
- go to a concert
- go hiking

Redewendungen und Grammatik: Das Wochenende beschreiben

a Ordnen Sie die Freizeitbeschäftigungen auf Seite 80 in fünf Gruppen ein.

At the weekend …
I always …	I usually … *normalerweise*	I often …	I sometimes … *manchmal*	I never …
go for a walk	meet friends	make a cake	go to the theatre	work in the garden
read the newspaper	go shopping	go hiking	go to a restaurant	go skiing
drink coffee	watch TV	write a Email	go to a concert	go to church
listen to musik	cook	phone	write a letter	go to a football match

b Arbeiten Sie mit jemandem zusammen, mit dem Sie sonst nicht zusammensitzen.
Unterhalten Sie sich über Ihr Wochenende. Notieren Sie sich in der Tabelle rechts, was Ihr Partner / Ihre Partnerin sagt.

A At the weekend I *(often write a letter)*.
What about you?
B I *(sometimes write a letter)*.
I *(never go skiing)*.
What about you?
A I *(never go skiing)*.

Yes	No
write a letter	go skiing
She goes to restaurant	hiking
goes to cinema	she doesn't go hiking
goes swimming	

c Berichten Sie der Klasse, was Ihr Partner / Ihre Partnerin gesagt hat.

A This is what *(Ingrid)* does at the weekend.
(She) *(writes a letter)*, and …, and …
(She) doesn't *(go skiing)*, and *(she)* doesn't …

Rückblick

In Units 16 – 19 haben Sie unter anderem gelernt, wie man …

… seine berufliche Tätigkeit beschreibt.
I work full-time/part-time.
I'm retired. / I'm a housewife.

… von seinem Tagesablauf erzählt.
I get up at six. I don't have a big breakfast.
I start work at eight o'clock.

… über seine Freizeit spricht.
In the evening I sometimes watch TV.
On Sunday I often visit friends.

… Vorlieben und Abneigungen beschreibt.
I like wine, but I don't like beer much. *(sehr)*
I don't mind the hot weather. *mir macht das heiße Wetter nichts aus / Ich merke das heiße Wetter nicht*

… über das Wetter spricht.
What's the weather like? *Wie ist das Wetter?*
It rains/snows a lot in the winter.

… Vorschläge macht.
Let's go to the market. – That's a nice idea. *Lassen Sie uns zum Markt gehn / Lasst uns zum Markt gehen*
Shall we go to the cathedral? – *sollen / Werden wir gehn*
I'd rather not. *I'd = I would / Ich würde nicht lieber nicht*

let's = let us = Lass uns

Shall we = Sollen wir   Should = Sollten

21 Do they speak English here?

Presentation

1a **In Funchal kauft Mary Postkarten.**

Track 79

INGE Postcards for your family, Mary?
MARY Yes. One for my grandsons, one for my granddaughters.
INGE Do you often see your family?
MARY Yes, I do. They all live nearby. *in der Nähe*
INGE That's nice.
MARY Do you and Bruno often see your daughter?
INGE No, we don't, I'm afraid. About *etwa* once a year. Boston is so far away. *einmal*

Practice

1b **Wie oft sehen Sie Ihre Familie?**

A Do you often *(see your son)*?
B Yes, I do. / No, I don't.
A How often *(do you see your son)*?
B About …

once *einmal*		day
twice *zweimal*		week
three times	a	week
four times		month
… times		year

see your son/daughter/children/ grandchildren • see your neighbour/ teacher • have a holiday • go for a meal • write a letter • make a cake • visit relatives • go to a concert / the theatre

Zusatzwortschatz

twice a week	*zweimal in der Woche*
three times a month	*dreimal im Monat*
four times a year	*viermal im Jahr*

Presentation

2a **Inge fragt Ann, ob sie Neuengland kennt.**

INGE Do you know Boston, Ann? Or New England?
ANN No, I don't. I know parts of the west coast quite well. Do you know California?
INGE Not very well. Now where's the shopkeeper?

Zusatzwortschatz

| I know … very well. | Ich kenne … sehr gut. |
| I don't know … very well. | Ich kenne … nicht sehr gut. |

Practice

2b **Welche Städte und Länder kennen Sie?**

A Do you know *(Berlin)*?
B Yes, I do. *(I know Berlin quite/very well.)* / No, I don't. *(I don't know Berlin very well.)*

Berlin • Hamburg • Munich • Dresden • London • Amsterdam • Austria • the USA • Switzerland • England • France • …

3a **Ob sie hier wohl Englisch und Deutsch sprechen?**

ANN What do you think? Do they speak English here?
INGE Yes, they do, I'm sure. Well, I'm sure they understand it. Is that the shopkeeper?
ANN I don't know. Let's ask.

3b **In einem Laden hängt dieses Schild. Welche Sprachen werden hier gesprochen?**

> English spoken
> On parle français
> Man spricht Deutsch

A Do they speak *(English)*?
B Yes, they do. / No, they don't.

English • Italian • German • Spanish • French • Dutch

4 **Hören Sie nun den gesamten Dialog.**

Information & Tips

Do they speak English?

Etwa 350 Millionen Menschen auf der Welt sprechen Englisch als Muttersprache – vor allem in den USA, in Großbritannien, Kanada, Australien, Irland, Neuseeland und Südafrika. Mindestens weitere 100 Millionen gebrauchen Englisch als zweite oder Amtssprache – z. B. in Ländern wie Indien, Pakistan, Bangladesch, den Philippinen, Nigeria und anderen afrikanischen Ländern.

Und mindestens weitere 100 Millionen Menschen sprechen Englisch als Fremdsprache. Englisch ist die weltweit wichtigste Sprache im Geschäftsleben, im internationalen Reiseverkehr (besonders in der Luftfahrt), in der Werbung, der Wissenschaft und im Computerwesen. Etwa 80 Prozent der in Computern gespeicherten Daten sind auf Englisch. Drei Viertel aller Briefe auf der Welt werden auf Englisch geschrieben.

Grammar

I speak German.	I **don't** speak Italian.	**Do** I speak French?
You speak German.	You **don't** speak Italian.	**Do** you speak French?
We speak German.	We **don't** speak Italian.	**Do** we speak French?
They speak German.	They **don't** speak Italian.	**Do** they speak French?

💡 In Unit 17 haben Sie gelernt, dass Aussagen mit I, you, we und they verneint werden, indem wir das Wort don't (do not) vor das Verb stellen (außer bei dem Verb be). Fragen werden gebildet, indem wir das Wort do vor I, you, we und they stellen.

Do I know Berlin?	Yes, I **do**.	No, I **don't**.
Do you know Berlin?	Yes, you **do**.	No, you **don't**.
Do we know Berlin?	Yes, we **do**.	No, we **don't**.
Do they know Berlin?	Yes, they **do**.	No, they **don't**.

💡 In Kurzantworten auf Fragen mit do wird do wiederholt. Die Kurzantworten lauten:
– Yes, … do. / – No, … don't.

Useful Phrases

Track 83

Do you often see your family?	Sehen Sie Ihre Familie oft?
About once a year.	Etwa einmal im Jahr.
Twice a year.	Zweimal im Jahr.
Three times a month.	Dreimal im Monat.
Boston is so far away.	Boston ist so weit weg.
Do you know California?	Kennen Sie Kalifornien?
I don't know.	Ich weiß (es) nicht.
I'm sure. *schon*	Ich bin (mir) sicher.
Let's ask.	Kommen Sie, wir fragen.

Exercises

1a Bringen Sie die Wörter in die richtige Reihenfolge, sodass sich Fragen ergeben.

1. you / Do / watch / TV – *Do you watch TV?* ?
2. you / it / every evening / watch / Do – *Do you watsch it every evening* ?
3. you / late / Do / get / on / Sunday / up – *Do you get up late on Sunday*
4. work / Do / full-time / you – *Do you work full-time* ?

1b Beantworten Sie nun die Fragen 1–4 mit **Yes, I do** oder **No, I don't**.

1. *Yes, I do*
2. *No, I don't*
3. *No, I don't*
4. *No, I don't*

Exercises

1c Und nun bilden Sie Fragen mit **Do you** und stellen Sie sie anderen Kursmitgliedern.

Verwenden Sie diese Stichwörter: speak Spanish? speak Italian?
go hiking? go to the cinema at the weekend?
make cakes? make jam?
have a big family? have a dog?

Do you ----

2 Ergänzen Sie.

		Land	Sprache			Land	Sprache
1	GB	Britain	English	4	USA	United States	*English*
2	A	*Australia*	German	5	I	Italy	*Italian*
3	F	France	*French*	6	E	*Spain*	Spanish

3a Ergänzen Sie die Fragen.

BRUNO & INGE	Times a week	Times a year
have a holiday		2
see their daughter		~~1~~
~~visit friends~~	~~1~~	
~~eat fish~~	~~2~~	
go shopping	~~3~~	
~~go to the theatre~~		~~3~~

1 How often do they *visit friends*? – About once a week.
2 How often do they *see their daughter*? – About once a year.
3 How often *do they go to the theatre*? – About three times a year.
4 How often *do they eat fish*? – About two times a week.
5 How often *do they go shopping*? – About three times a week.
6 How often *do they have a holiday*? – About twice a year.

3b Und nun stellen Sie einem Kursmitglied die Fragen 3–6. How often do you .....

4 Wissen Sie noch, wie es heißt?
1 Sehen Sie Ihre Familie oft? *Do you often see your family?*
2 Sprechen sie hier Englisch? *Do they speak English here?*
3 Was meinen Sie? *What do you think?*
4 Ich bin sicher, dass sie Englisch verstehen. *I'm sure they understand English*
5 Kennen Sie Boston? *Do you know Boston?*

22 Does she speak English?

Presentation

1a Ann und Inge unterhalten sich über ihre Kinder.

Track 84

INGE   Is this your son and his wife?
ANN   Yes.
INGE   Does he miss England?
ANN   No, he doesn't. He likes it in Bavaria.
INGE   Does his wife speak English?
ANN   Yes, she does. But I'm afraid we don't get on very well.
INGE   Oh dear, I'm sorry. Does that make things very difficult when you see them?
ANN   Yes, it does, I'm afraid. And you? Do you and Bruno get on well with your son-in-law?
INGE   Yes, we do. We're very lucky. Bruno likes Glenn a lot.
ANN   Does Glenn speak German?
INGE   No, he doesn't.
ANN   Well, you and Bruno speak English, so that's no problem. Does your daughter miss Germany?
INGE   No, she doesn't. But I miss her sometimes. She's very happy in America. She wants to stay there.

Practice

1b **Yes, he/she does** oder **No, he/she doesn't**?

1. Does Ann's son live in Germany?
2. Does he like it there?
3. Does her daughter-in-law speak English?
4. Does Ann get on well with her?
5. Does Ann say why?
6. Does Inge get on well with Glenn?
7. Does Bruno get on well with Glenn?
8. Does his son-in-law speak German?
9. Does Inge's daughter miss Germany?

1c Wählen Sie eine weibliche Person, die Sie gut kennen. Ihr/e Nachbar/in stellt Ihnen zu dieser Person vier Fragen.

A   Fragen Sie mich nach *(meiner Tochter)*.
B   Does she live in …?
       … she work full-time?
       … she like …?
       … she speak …?

1d Und nun wechseln Sie. Ihr/e Nachbar/in wählt eine männliche Person. Sie stellen die vier Fragen mit **Does he …?**

Presentation

2a Inge zeigt einige Fotos.

INGE Look. This is a photo of her.
ANN Oh, isn't she pretty?
INGE And this is Glenn. Look at him.
 I like him in that hat.
ANN Yes. Isn't it nice?
INGE This is a photo of us in …
 Oh, I can't remember the name
 of the place now. I must ask
 them when I see them again.

Zusatzwortschatz

jacket	Jacke, Jackett
skirt	Rock
shirt	Hemd
pair of trousers	Hose
smart	chic
unusual	ungewöhnlich

Practice

2b Was gefällt Ihnen an der Kleidung der anderen Kursmitglieder?

A Look at *(Ingrid/Günther)*.

I like	her / him	in that	pullover. / dress. / jacket. / pair of trousers. / blouse. / skirt. / shirt.

B Yes, …

… isn't	he / she / it	nice? / lovely? / pretty? / smart? / unusual? / funny?

---

3 Hören Sie nun den gesamten Dialog.

Information & Tips

Britisches und amerikanisches Englisch

Es gibt verschiedene Formen oder Varianten des Englischen, so wie es z. B. im Deutschen Hochdeutsch und Schwyzerdütsch gibt. Die beiden wichtigsten Varianten sind britisches Englisch (BE) und amerikanisches Englisch (AE). Briten und Amerikaner haben in der Regel keinerlei Probleme einander zu verstehen, d. h. Sie werden mit dem Englisch, das Sie jetzt lernen, überall gleich gut verstanden werden.
Einige Unterschiede gibt es aber. Hauptsächlich liegen sie in der Aussprache, aber auch bei der Schreibweise bestimmter Wörter (z. B. BE centre = AE center) gibt es Unterschiede. Zum Teil werden für dieselben Dinge andere Wörter gebraucht (z. B. heißt Wohnung im BE flat, im AE aber apartment, Benzin im BE petrol, im AE aber gas). Die wenigsten Unterschiede gibt es in der Grammatik.

lucky – happy

Im Dialog heißt es We're very lucky und She's very happy. Lucky und happy haben beide mit Glück zu tun. We're very lucky entspricht „Wir haben viel Glück", d. h. das Schicksal war uns wohl gesonnen und alles ist gut gegangen. She's very happy entspricht „Sie ist sehr glücklich", d. h. sie hat ein Gefühl von Freude und Zufriedenheit.

Grammar

He speaks English.	He **doesn't** speak German.	**Does** he speak French?
She misses her friends.	She **doesn't** miss the carnival.	**Does** she miss you?
It rains.	It **doesn't** rain much.	**Does** it snow?

💡 Erinnern Sie sich? In Unit 19 haben Sie gelernt, dass Aussagen in der 3. Person (nach he, she, it, Ann, the concert usw.) verneint werden, indem wir doesn't (does not) vor das Verb stellen. Fragen werden gebildet, indem wir does an den Satzanfang stellen.

Does he speak French?	Yes, he **does**.	No, he **doesn't**.
Does she miss you?	Yes, she **does**.	No, she **doesn't**.
Does it snow?	Yes, it **does**.	No, it **doesn't**.

💡 In der Kurzantwort wird does aus der Frage wiederholt: – Yes, … does. / – No, … doesn't.

I know. Ask **me**. Give **me** the letter.	
You know. I'll ask **you**. I'll give **you** the letter.	
He knows. Ask **him**. Give **him** the letter.	
She knows. Ask **her**. Give **her** the letter.	
We know. Ask **us**. Give **us** the letter.	
You know. I'll ask **you**. I'll give **you** the letter.	
They know. Ask **them**. Give **them** the letter.	

💡
me	mich, mir
you	dich, dir; Sie, Ihnen
him	ihn, ihm
her	sie, ihr
us	uns
you	euch; Sie, Ihnen
them	sie, ihnen

Useful Phrases

Track 87

We don't get on very well.	*Wir kommen nicht gut miteinander aus.*
We're very lucky.	*Wir haben viel Glück.*
That's no problem.	*Das ist kein Problem.*
I like him in that hat.	*Ich mag ihn mit dem Hut.*
Isn't it nice?	*Ist es nicht schön?*

Exercises

1a Beantworten Sie die Fragen mit **Yes, he/she/it does** oder **No, he/she/it doesn't**.

1. Does Inge live in Cologne? (Unit 1)
2. Does Ann speak German? (Unit 3)
3. Does Bruno drink beer? (Unit 6)
4. Does Bruno know Rolf Mayer? (Unit 7)
5. Does Ann's son live in Munich? (Unit 9)
6. Does Ann live in Oxford? (Unit 12)
7. Does Mary have two grandsons? (Unit 13)
8. Does the ship stop in Tangier? (Unit 14)
9. Does Ann get up at 7 o'clock? (Unit 16)
10. Does Inge have a big lunch? (Unit 17)
11. Does Ann's son sing? (Unit 18)
12. Does Ann mind the cold? (Unit 19)

1b Vorschlag für eine Hausaufgabe: Sehen Sie sich die bisherigen Units an und bilden Sie Fragen zu den Charakteren, die Sie dann in der nächsten Kursstunde der Klasse stellen.

Exercises

2a Stellen Sie passende Fragen mit does.

1 When does *Inge watch TV with Bruno* ? – On Friday.
2 When does ....? – On Sunday.
3 When ....? – On Thursday.
4 When ....? – On Saturday.
5 When ....? – On Tuesday.

Inge's week	
Sunday	*She writes an email to Anke.*
Monday	
Tuesday	*She goes to her English class.*
Wednesday	
Thursday	*She meets friends for a drink.*
Friday	~~She watches TV with Bruno.~~
Saturday	*She goes shopping.*

2b Alle schreiben auf, was sie regelmäßig an einem bestimmten Wochentag machen.

Zum Beispiel schreibt *(Ingrid)* auf einen Zettel: *I play "Doppelkopf" on Wednesday.*
Geben Sie den Zettel mit Ihrem Satz Ihrer Platznachbarin / Ihrem Platznachbarn.
Sie/Er berichtet der Klasse, was Sie geschrieben haben, ohne den Tag zu nennen.
Beispiel: *(Ingrid) plays "Doppelkopf".*

Die Klasse muss durch Fragen den Tag herausbekommen.
Beispiel: *When does (Ingrid) play "Doppelkopf"? On Monday? – No, not on Monday.*
Does she play on Tuesday? – No, not on Tuesday.
Does she play on Wednesday? – Yes, she does.

3 Kreuzworträtsel.

down ↓ (senkrecht)
2 *My* name's Ann. What's your name?
4 Bruno and I don't see *our* daughter often.
5 Come and visit *us* when you are in Germany.
7 I don't see my grandchildren very often. I miss *___m*.

across → (waagerecht)
1 I know Sonia's husband well. Do you know *him*?
3 When will I see *you* again?
6 I know Paris well. Do you know *it*?
8 We're on one of the photos. Yes, this is the photo of *us*.
9 Do you miss your daughter? – Yes, I miss *her* sometimes.
10 Excuse *me*. What's the time, please?

23 I'm sorry. – That's all right.

Presentation

Track 88

1a **Mary fragt jemanden, ob er zum Bowlingverein gehört.**
MARY Excuse me. Are you with the German bowling club?
MAN No, I'm afraid not.
MARY Oh, I'm sorry.
MAN That's all right.

Practice

1b **Üben Sie, wie man sich entschuldigt und auf eine Entschuldigung reagiert.**
A Excuse me. *(Is this the French class?)*
B No, I'm afraid not.
A Oh, I'm sorry.
B That's all right.

Is this the French class? • Are you the English teacher? • Is this the Bristol Hotel? • Are you from Italy? • Are you Hannah Schulz? • Do you work here? • Are you from the USA? • Are you with that … club?

Presentation

2a **Mary fragt noch jemanden.**

Track 89

MARY   Excuse me. Are you with the German bowling club?
MAN   Yes, I am.
MARY   Oh good. Can you help me, please? I'm looking for Inge and Bruno's cabin. Do you know which number it is?
MAN   Yes, it's cabin number 337.
MARY   Thank you.
MAN   They're packing at the moment. Or rather, Inge is packing, and Bruno is helping. He's finishing the last bottle of Madeira wine and singing to her.
MARY   Oh!

Zusatzwortschatz

room number 5	Zimmer Nummer 5
20 Wood Street	Holzstraße 20

Practice

2b **Sagen Sie diese Zahlen.**

101	a/one hundred and one
212	two hundred and twelve
323	three hundred and twenty-three
457	four hundred and fifty-seven
999	nine hundred and ninety-nine
1000	a/one thousand

100, 137, 248, 362, 473, 587, 614, 725, 864

2c **Üben Sie die Zahlen im Gespräch.**

A   Excuse me.
    Is this *(cabin number twenty-one)*?
B   No, I'm afraid not. It's number *(twenty-two)*.

cabin number 21 (22) • cabin number 45 (46) • house number 69 (70) • house number 122 (124) • 165 Museum Street (167) • 182 Museum Street (184) • room number 657 (637) • room number 942 (940) • room number 535 (525)

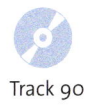

---

3 **Hören Sie nun den gesamten Dialog.**

Track 90

Information & Tips

Excuse me – I'm sorry

Beide Redewendungen entsprechen im Deutschen „Entschuldigung" oder „Entschuldigen Sie". Excuse me sagt man, bevor man etwas macht oder fragt, z. B. Excuse me, what's the time, please? Dagegen sagt man I'm sorry, um sich zu entschuldigen, nachdem man etwas getan hat. Mary entschuldigt sich bei dem Fremden mit I'm sorry, weil sie fälschlicherweise angenommen hatte, dass er zu Brunos Bowlingverein gehört.

Auf eine Entschuldigung mit I'm sorry kann man mit That's all right (Keine Ursache. / Schon gut.) antworten.
Nicht vergessen: I'm sorry bedeutet auch „Es/Das tut mir Leid", z. B. Mary's not very well this morning. – Oh, I'm sorry.

Zahlen

Achten Sie darauf, dass bei Zahlen über 100 im britischen Englisch and gebraucht werden muss, z. B. a hundred and twenty-five. Im amerikanischen Englisch kann and weggelassen werden.

Grammar

I'm	pack**ing** at the moment.	
You're	pack**ing** at the moment.	
He's	pack**ing** at the moment.	
She's	pack**ing** at the moment.	
We're	pack**ing** at the moment.	
You're	pack**ing** at the moment.	
They're	pack**ing** at the moment.	

hav**e**	–	hav**ing**	phon**e** – phon**ing**	
liv**e**	–	liv**ing**	writ**e** – writ**ing**	
com**e**	–	com**ing**		

- Diese Form setzt sich zusammen aus einer Form von be (am, are oder is) und einem Verb mit der Endung -ing.
- Mit dieser Form beschreiben wir etwas, das im Augenblick nicht abgeschlossen ist und gerade verläuft – daher der Name „Verlaufsform".
- Wenn ein Verb auf -e endet, fällt dieses -e vor -ing weg.

Useful Phrases

Track 91

Excuse me.	*Entschuldigung. / Entschuldigen Sie.*
I'm sorry.	*Entschuldigung. / Entschuldigen Sie.*
That's all right.	*Das ist in Ordnung. / Macht nichts. / Keine Ursache. / Schon gut.*
They're packing.	*Sie packen.*
Or rather, Inge's packing.	*Das heißt, Inge packt.*

[handwritten note: rather = das heißt, oder eigentlich = ziemlich, eher, lieber, vielmehr]

Exercises

1 Spielen Sie Bingo mit Zahlen bis 99.
(Spielanleitung siehe S. 37.)

2 Schreiben Sie diese Zahlen als Wort aus.

A 15 _fifteen_ D 46 _forty six_
B 12 _twelve_ E 53 _fifty three_
C 97 _ninety seven_ F 13 _thirteen_

3a Wählen Sie aus diesen drei Zahlenreihen eine aus und lesen Sie sie ihrem Partner / Ihrer Partnerin vor. Er/Sie muss herausfinden, welche Sie vorgelesen haben.

A	50	15	15
B	15	50	15
C	50	15	50

*[handwritten:
fifty fifteen fifteen
fifteen fifty fifteen
fifty fifteen fifty]*

3b Tauschen Sie die Rollen und denken Sie sich noch weitere Reihen aus.

Exercises

4 Kreuzworträtsel

1. My husband has a part-time job. He is _working_ this afternoon.
2. I'm here at home. I'm _listening_ to a concert on the radio.
3. We are _staying_ in a lovely hotel near the cathedral.
4. What are you _doing_?
5. I'm _writing_ an email to a friend.
6. We're _drinking_ cappuccino in a café near the market.
7. I'm so tired. I'm _going_ to bed.

Crossword answer (across): **READING**

Down answers: 1. working, 2. listening, 3. staying, 4. doing, 5. writing, 6. drinking, 7. going

5 Ordnen Sie den Sätzen die richtigen Buchstaben zu und ergänzen Sie die richtige Form des Verbs.

1. Can you help me, please? — **B**
2. Can Ann phone her son? — **D**
3. Can David go and buy some bread? — **A**
4. Can Craig and Alexander come to the cinema? — **E**
5. Can you and Silvia help me with this postcard in German? — **C**

A. Sorry. He _is cooking_ lunch at the moment. (cook)
B. Sorry. I _am working_ at the moment. (work)
C. Sorry. We _are making_ breakfast at the moment. (make)
D. Sorry. She _is phoning_ Mary at the moment. (phone)
E. Sorry. They _are looking_ for their dog at the moment. (look)

24 Goodbye

Presentation

1a **Ann bittet Inge um ihre Adresse.**

ANN Inge, let me have your address.
INGE It's In den Hüppen 26, 53879 Euskirchen.
ANN Can you spell the name of the street, please?
INGE Of course. It's "in", new word "den", D E N, new word "Hüppen", H U-umlaut double P E N.
ANN In den Hüppen. That's a funny name.
INGE Yes, it is. I often have to spell it for German people, too.
ANN And what's the postcode for Euskirchen again?
INGE 53879.
ANN 53879. OK, thank you.

Zusatzwortschatz

ä = a-umlaut   Das komplette englische Alphabet finden Sie auf Seite 96.
ß = double s

Practice

1b **Sprechen Sie diese Buchstaben nach.**

A H J K
B C D E G P T V
F L M N S X Z
I Y
Q U W

1c **Üben Sie das Buchstabieren.**

A What's *(your name)*, please?
B It's *(Schmitz)*.
A Can you spell that, please?
B Yes, it's *(SCHMITZ)*.
A Thank you.

your name • the name of your street • the name of your town • your neighbour's name

Presentation

2a **Ann möchte die Telefonnummer haben.** *(Track 93)*

ANN And what's your telephone number, please?
INGE It's 02251 – that's the code – and the number is 34529.
ANN 02251–34529. OK.
INGE And what's your address and phone number, Ann?
ANN Here they are – on this piece of paper.
INGE Thank you.

3a **Es ist Zeit zum Verabschieden.** *(Track 94)*

INGE Well, it's time to say goodbye. Goodbye, Mary. It was lovely to meet you.
MARY Goodbye, Inge.
INGE When you visit your son, Ann, you must come and visit us for a few days.
ANN I'd love to see you again. You and Bruno must come and have a holiday in England. In the summer, Bruno, when it's warm.
BRUNO Well, we want to visit Anke in Boston next year. Perhaps we'll fly via London.

4 **Hören Sie nun den gesamten Dialog.** *(Track 95)*

Practice

2b **Fragen Sie nach Telefonnummern.**

A What's *(your)* telephone number, please?
B It's …
A And what's the code?
B It's …

*your • your neighbour's •
your best friend's •
your son's/daughter's/brother's/…*

3b **Üben Sie, sich zu verabschieden.**

A Well, it's time to say goodbye. It was lovely to meet you.
B When you *(come to Germany)*, you must come and visit me. I'd love to see you again.
A Thank you. That's very nice of you.

*come to Germany/Austria/Switzerland •
come to Berlin/Salzburg/Zurich/… •
come to my part of Germany/Austria/
Switzerland • are near …straße*

Information & Tips

Das ist im amerikanischen Englisch anders.
Im amerikanischen Englisch wird der Buchstabe Z genau wie das deutsche Wort „sie" ausgesprochen. Die Ziffer 0 (Null) in Telefonnummern spricht man als Buchstabe O (wie das Wort Oh) oder als zero.
In Großbritannien ist es üblich, die einzelnen Zahlen von Telefonnummern anzugeben, z. B. 39 24 26 = three nine two four two six.

Die Postleitzahl heißt im amerikanischen Englisch zip code, nicht postcode. Übrigens: In Großbritannien setzt sich die Postleitzahl aus Buchstaben und Ziffern zusammen: London SE8 7LN. In den USA ist es eine fünfstellige Zahl. Ihr werden zwei Buchstaben für den Bundesstaat vorangestellt: z. B. CA 95814 (CA = California), NY 10010 (NY = New York).

Grammar

Track 96

Das Alphabet

Hören Sie sich die Aussprache des Alphabets auf der CD an.

A	B	C	D	E	F	G	H	I	J	K	L	M
N	O	P	Q	R	S	T	U	V	W	X	Y	Z

Useful Phrases

Track 97

Can you spell that, please?	*Können Sie das bitte buchstabieren?*
What's your address?	*Wie ist Ihre Adresse?*
What's your telephone number?	*Wie ist Ihre Telefonnummer?*
What's the postcode for Euskirchen?	*Wie lautet die Postleitzahl für Euskirchen?*
It's time to say goodbye.	*Es ist Zeit, Auf Wiedersehen zu sagen.*
When you come to Germany,	*Wenn Sie nach Deutschland kommen,*
you must come and visit us for a few days.	*müssen Sie uns ein paar Tage besuchen.*
It was lovely to meet you.	*Es war sehr schön, Sie kennen zu lernen.*

Exercises

1a Ihr/e Kursleiter/in spricht jeweils einen Buchstaben aus jedem der folgenden Paare vor. Welchen Buchstaben? Kreisen Sie ein.

1 M or N?   4 A or H?   7 U or W?
2 B or P?   5 E or I?   8 V or W?
3 D or T?   6 I or Y?   9 G or J?

1b Welche Buchstaben reimen sich? Ordnen Sie aus dem Kasten zu.

1 F, L, ___, ___, ___

2 B, C, D, ___, G, ___, ___, V

3 A, H, J, ___

4 I, ___

5 Q, ___, W

> E, K, M, N, P, S, T, U, Y

2 **Who, how** oder **what**?

1 .... is your telephone number?
2 .... are you this morning?
3 .... is the man over there?
4 .... is he like? – Very nice.
5 .... is "fly" in German?
6 .... cold is it in Germany now?
7 .... is your address, please?

Exercises

3 Ordnen Sie die Sätze so, dass sich ein Gespräch ergibt.

- [ ] Yes, it's B R U-umlaut H L.
- [ ] Yes, I do. Can I help you?
- [1] Excuse me. Do you speak English?
- [ ] Can you spell the name of the hotel, please?
- [ ] Mährengasse. That's M A-umlaut H R E N G A double S E.
- [ ] Yes. I'm looking for the Hotel Brühl.
- [ ] Sorry. What's the name of the street again?
- [ ] Oh, Brühl. That's in Mährengasse.
- [ ] Ah, now I understand. Thank you.

4 Ordnen Sie zu.

1. What's your address, please?
2. You can stay with us.
3. Can you spell that, please?
4. I'd love to visit Germany.

A. Well, why don't you come and visit us in Ulm?
B. Yes, of course. H I G H B U R Y.
C. Are you sure that's no problem?
D. It's 28 Highbury Road.

5 Kreuzworträtsel

down ↓ (senkrecht)

1. I'd _ _ _ _ _ _ to see you again.
2. Come and _ _ _ _ _ for a few days.
3. The _ _ _ _ _ _ for Euskirchen is 02251.
5. In den Hüppen is a _ _ _ _ _ _ _ name for a street.
6. The _ _ _ _ _ code for Euskirchen is 53879.
10. We want _ _ _ visit Anke next year.

across → (waagerecht)

1. This is our _ _ _ _ _ _ meal. Tomorrow I'll be at home again.
4. Perhaps we'll fly to Boston _ _ _ _ _ London.
5. You must come and visit us for a _ _ _ _ _ days.
6. What's your tele _ _ _ _ _ _ _ number, please?
7. And what's _ _ _ _ _ _ address?
8. Can you _ _ _ _ _ _ _ the name of the street, please?
9. I'm _ _ _ _ from the USA. I'm from Britain.
11. Perhaps we'll _ _ _ _ via London.

25 Revision

Das Alphabet

a **Alle Kursmitglieder arbeiten zusammen.**
Ein Kursmitglied beginnt und sagt A. Der Reihe nach sagen die anderen das Alphabet weiter: B, C, D usw. Wenn ein Fehler gemacht wird, beginnen Sie wieder bei A.

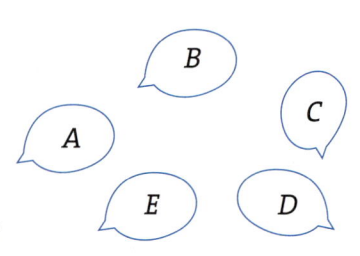

b **Suchen Sie sich mit einem Partner / einer Partnerin vier längere Wörter aus den Units 21–24.**
Schreiben Sie sie in die linke Spalte. Setzen Sie sich dann mit einem anderen Paar zusammen. Buchstabieren Sie Ihre Wörter dem anderen Paar. Das andere Paar buchstabiert Ihnen seine vier Wörter. Schreiben Sie sie auf.

....
....
....
....

Die Zahlen

Spielen Sie Bingo.
Jedes Kursmitglied wählt sich neun der rechts stehenden Zahlen aus und schreibt sie in beliebiger Reihenfolge auf seiner Bingokarte auf. (Weiteres Vorgehen wie in der Spielanleitung auf S. 37.)

101 - 167 - 213 - 298 - 326 - 344 - 409 - 475 - 516 - 560 - 613 - 630 - 719 - 790 - 847 - 874 - 969 - 996

Redewendungen

Welche Redewendung passt zu den folgenden Dialogen?

Excuse me. • *I'm sorry.* • *I'm afraid not.* • *Oh dear.* • *That's all right* • *Here you are* • *Of course.*

1 A Are you the English teacher?
   B No, I'm not.
   A (Entschuldigung.) ... _I'm sorry_
   B (Keine Ursache.) ... _That's all right_

2 A (Entschuldigen Sie.) ... What's the time?
   B It's five past ten.
      Excuse me

3 A We have a very noisy room.
   B (O je.) ... _Oh dear_

4 A Can you help me this afternoon?
   B (Leider nicht.) ... _I'm afraid not_

5 A Can I have the sugar, please?
   B (Natürlich.) ... _Yes of course_
      (Bitte schön.) ... _Here you are_

Grammatik: Fragen mit do und does

a Arbeiten Sie mit einem anderen Kursmitglied zusammen.
Formulieren Sie sinnvolle Fragen zu den Antworten.

1 Do ....? Yes, I do.
2 Do ....? No, I don't.
3 Does ....? Yes, she does.
4 Does ....? No, he doesn't.
5 Does ....? No, she doesn't.
6 Does ....? Yes, he does.

b Stellen Sie nun Ihre Fragen anderen Kursmitgliedern.
(Reihenfolge der Fragen unbedingt verändern.)

Grammatik: Fragen mit does

In diesem Ratespiel sucht sich ein Kursmitglied ein anderes aus, ohne aber diese Person zu nennen.
Alle anderen müssen herausfinden, wer die Person ist, indem sie Fragen mit does stellen.

Hier ein Beispiel:

A My person is a woman.
B Does your person live here in *(Berlin)*?
A Yes, she does.
C Does she like the heat?
A No, she doesn't.
D Is it *(Ingrid)*?
A Yes, it is.

*live • come from • get up at… •
go shopping on… • speak • like •
cook • sing • go to the theatre/cinema •
go hiking • go swimming • work…*

Rückblick

In den letzten Units haben Sie unter anderem gelernt, wie man …

… fragt, wie oft etwas geschieht. Do you often see your family? – No, I don't.

… fragt, ob jemand Deutsch/Englisch spricht. Do you speak German/English? – Yes, I do.
auch: can you speak ...

… sich entschuldigt. Oh, I'm sorry. – That's all right.

… jemanden bittet, etwas zu buchstabieren. Can you spell that, please?

… etwas buchstabiert. That's M U-umlaut double L E R.

… nach einer Postleitzahl/Telefonnummer fragt. What's the postcode/telephone number, please?
what's your ...

… sich verabschiedet. Goodbye. It was lovely to meet you. When you're in Germany, you must come and visit us.

Are you good at baking?

Home Practice

Unit 1

1 Am, is oder are? Verwenden Sie nur Langformen.

1. Hello, my name ...is... Frank.
2. Where ...are... you from, Frank?
3. I ...am... from Bregenz.
4. I ...am... not from Switzerland. I ...am... from Austria.
5. ...Are... you from England? – Yes, I ...am... .

2 Wie antwortet Jack: Yes, I am oder No, I'm not?

1. Are you Mr Brown? – Jack: No, I'm not
2. Are you from Canada? – Jack: No, I'm not
3. Are you from Britain? – Jack: Yes, I am
4. Are you from Scotland? – Jack: No, I'm not
5. Are you from England? – Jack: Yes, I am

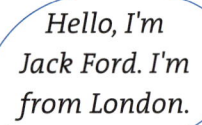

Hello, I'm Jack Ford. I'm from London.

Unit 2

Ergänzen Sie aus dem Kasten.

you • He's • Her • ~~you~~ • His • I'm • my • She's

SUSAN Hello, ...my...¹ name is Susan.
KARIN And ...I'm...² Karin.
SUSAN Nice to meet ...you...³, Karin.
       Where are ...you...⁴ from?
KARIN Germany.
SUSAN Really? I have a son in Germany, in Paderborn.
       ...He's...⁵ a computer expert.
       ...His...⁶ wife is from the USA.
       ...Her...⁷ name is Mary-Ann.
       ...She's...⁸ nice.

Unit 3

Schreiben Sie die Sätze an die richtige Stelle.

> Is that right?
> Yes, I can.
> Can you speak English?
> Yes, that's right.
> What's the name of this street?

A Excuse me. _Can you speak English?_
B _Yes, I can_ A little.
A Oh good. _What's the name of this street?_
B It's Lenzstraße.
A Lenzstraße. _Is that right_
B _Yes, that's right_

Unit 4

1 Welche Gebäude/Einrichtungen sind gemeint?

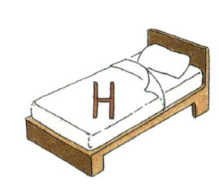

bar   _hotel_   _restaurant_   _museum_

2 Ordnen Sie die Wörter so, dass sich daraus Sätze ergeben.

1 surname / is / Inge's / Schmitz
   Inge's surname is Schmitz.

2 husband's first name / Bruno / is / Her
   Her husband's first name is Bruno.

3 member / club / He / is / of / a / bowling / a
   He is a member of a bowling club.

4 What's / name / club / of / the / the
   What's the name of the club ?

5 The / of / address / my / hotel / is / Museum Street, London
   The address of my hotel is Museum Street, London.

6 name / my / of / choir / The / is / Allegro Vivace
   The name of my choir is Allegro Vivace.

3 Wählen und ergänzen Sie.

I'm (in/with) ...in... the bar
(from/of) ...of... a nice hotel
(of/near) ...near... London. I'm here
(near/with) ...with... my British friend Alex.
He's (from/near) ...from... Scotland.

4a Welches Wort passt jeweils nicht zu den anderen drei? Kreisen Sie es ein.

1 grandson	brother	(daughter)	son
2 See you later.	Goodbye.	Bye-bye.	(Hello.)
3 (street)	member	teacher	neighbour

4b Und nun ergänzen Sie passende Wörter. Es gibt mehr als eine Möglichkeit.

1 hotel	restaurant	...bar...
2 husband	wife	...son...
3 English	French	...Spanish...
4	....	....

Unit 6

1 Kreuzworträtsel: my, your, his, her, our

across ⟶ (waagerecht)

1 _his_ first name is Tony.

   _my_ surname is Black.

2 I'm a member of a choir.

   The name of _the_ choir is Allegro Vivace.

4 We're OK. _our_ hotel is very good.

down ↓ (senkrecht)

1 This is Ann, and this is _her_ friend Mary.

3 How is _your_ husband this morning? –
   He's fine, thank you.

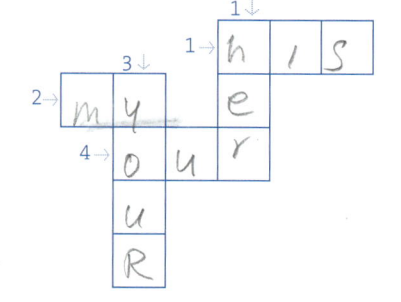

2 Welcher Ausdruck passt jeweils nicht zu den anderen drei? Kreisen Sie ihn ein.

1 Good morning.	Goodbye.	Good afternoon.	Good evening.
2 Fine, thanks.	OK.	Not very well.	Yes, please.
3 water	coffee	wine	tea

Unit 7

1 They're oder their?

Jack and Alison are from the USA. *They're* in Germany now. *They're* with *their* son and *their* daughter-in-law, Karin. *They're* in Garmisch-Partenkirchen now, in *their* hotel. Karin is from Garmisch. She is German.

2 Was wissen Sie noch? Ordnen Sie den Fragen die Antworten zu, indem Sie die Buchstaben A bis H in die Kästchen schreiben.

1. Is Bruno here with his bowling club? [C]
2. Are Bruno and Inge from Hamburg? [E]
3. Is Ann's surname Thomas? [A]
4. Is Inge's daughter in the USA? [B]
5. Is Mary married now? [H]
6. Is Ann's son in Cologne? [D]
7. Is Bruno Bruno Braun? [F]
8. Are the Mayers in Bruno's club? [G]

A Yes, it is.
B Yes, she is.
C Yes, he is.
D No, he isn't.
E No, they aren't.
F No, he isn't.
G Yes, they are.
H No, she isn't.

3 Beantworten Sie diese Fragen zu Übung 1 mit Yes, they are oder No, they aren't.

1. Are Jack and Alison from the USA? *Yes, they are*
2. Are they in the USA now? *No, they aren't*
3. Are they in a hotel? *Yes, they are*
4. Are they with their son? *Yes, they are*
5. Are their son and daughter-in-law both American? *No, they aren't. Their daughter-in-law is from German(y). Their son is American.*

4 Ergänzen Sie das Fragewort How, What, Where oder Who.

1. *Where* are Inge and Bruno from? – From Euskirchen.
2. *What* 's their surname? – It's Schmitz.
3. *Who* is Mary? – She's Ann's friend. (hu) wer
4. *How* is Mary this morning? – She's not very well. hau (wie)

Unit 8
Bezeichnen diese Wörter nur Männer, nur Frauen oder Männer und Frauen?

~~brothers~~
~~daughters~~
~~daughters-in-law~~
~~Englishmen~~
~~friends~~
~~Germans~~
~~grandsons~~
~~husbands~~
~~members~~
~~neighbours~~
~~sisters~~
~~teachers~~
~~wives~~

men (left circle): brothers, Englishmen, grandsons, husbands

friends (middle): Germans, members, neighbours, teachers

women (right circle): daughters, daughter-in-law, sisters, wives

Unit 9
Ergänzen Sie die richtigen Formen von (not) be.

1 Bruno isn't a member of a choir. He _is_ in a bowling club!
2 Inge's daughter _isn't_ in New York. She _lives (is)_ near Boston.
3 Ann and Mary _are_ both single. They _aren't_ married.
4 Ann: I can speak German, but I _am not_ German. I _am_ British.
5 Inge and Bruno: We _aren't_ from Euskirchen originally.
  We _are_ from Mannheim and Magdeburg originally.

Unit 11
Some, any oder a?

1 There are _some_ interesting clubs in Ashford, but there aren't _any_ carnival clubs.
2 I have _a_ nice cabin. There are _some_ very nice cabins here.
3 There are _some_ German people in the group, but there aren't _any_ English people.
4 There aren't _any_ nice dresses in this shop.
5 There's _a_ hotel with _a_ very good restaurant in Ashford Street.
6 There aren't _any_ young people in my club.
7 There isn't _any_ beer, but there is _some_ wine.
8 There's _some_ bread, but there isn't _any_ butter.
9 There's _some_ water here for you.

Unit 12
Schreiben Sie Fragen mit Would you like … oder Would you like to …

1 (some juice) Would you like some juice?
 – Not just now, thank you.
2 (coffee) Would you like some coffee? – Yes, please.
3 (visit me in Germany) Would you like to visit me in Germany?
 – Oh, lovely.
4 (the butter) Would you like the butter?
 – No, thank you.
5 (come and meet Angela) Would you like to come and meet Angela?
 – Later perhaps.

Unit 13
Have oder has?

1 This music group ..has.. a funny name.
2 We ..have.. some relatives in Canada.
3 The club ..has.. 26 members altogether. *altogether = zusammen*
4 There's a hotel in the village, and it ..has.. a very good restaurant.
5 A lot of the towns ..have.. some beautiful old buildings.
6 Oxford ..has.. about 35 colleges.
7 Our son and daughter-in-law ..have.. five children.
8 Our class ..has.. a teacher from England.
9 A married man ..has.. a wife. Married women ..have.. a husband.
 women

Unit 14
Flugzeug
Ordnen Sie die Wörter so, dass sich Sätze ergeben.

1 next / plane / The / at / six / o'clock / leaves
 The next plane leaves at six o'clock.
2 time / it / is / What
 What time is it ?
3 next / is / the / train / When
 When is the next train ?
4 much / we / have / time / How / in / London / will
 How much time will we have in London ?

Unit 16
Schreiben Sie die Wochentage.

1 S _ T _ R _ A Y
2 S _ _ _ A _
3 _ _ _ S _ A _
4 _ _ _ _ R S _ A _
5 F R I _ A _
6 W _ d _ _ _ S _ A _
7 _ _ o _ _ A _

```
June
19 Monday
20 Tuesday
21 Wednesday
22 Thursday
23 Friday
24 Saturday
25 Sunday
```

Unit 17
Ordnen Sie zu und entscheiden Sie, ob das Verb in der Klammer mit oder ohne don't stehen muss.

1 I often listen to the radio,   [D]
2 We don't arrive in the evening.   [ ]
3 They live in London.   [ ]
4 I speak English.   [ ]
5 I start work late,   [ ]
6 I like the theatre,   [ ]
7 We get up early on Saturday,   [ ]
8 I always drink tea for breakfast.   [E]

A They (live) .... in the USA.
B I (speak) .Sp............ Spanish, too.
C but we (get up) .... late on Sunday.
D but I (watch) *don't watch* TV.
E I (like) .do........... coffee with my breakfast.
F and I (finish) .... late, too.
G We (arrive) .... in the afternoon.
H but I (like) .do....like.. the cinema much.

Unit 18
Ordnen Sie zu und ergänzen Sie die richtige Form des Verbs (mit oder ohne -s).

1 We (live) .... in Museum Street.   [D]
2 Ann's daughter-in-law (sing) .... in a choir.   [ ]
3 Ann and Inge (speak) ....speak...... English.   [ ]
4 Ann (work) .... full-time.   [ ]
5 My husband and I (like) .....like..... Spain.   [ ]

A Her husband (do) .... a lot of sport.
B She (work) .... in Oxford.
C We often (go) .... there in the spring.
D Our friends (live) .... in Museum Street, too.
E They both (speak) .... German, too.

Unit 19
What oder how?

1 .... is the climate like?
2 .... old are they?
3 .... many people are there?
4 ...what... is a typical day for you?
5 I like Paris. .... about you?
6 .... are you? – Fine, thanks.

Unit 21
Bilden Sie Paare.

1 ....big.... – ....small....
2 .... – ....
3 .... – ....
4 .... – ....
5 .... – ....
6 .... – ....
7 .... – ....

letter – far away – I'm sure – often – twice – stop – big

never – nearby – small – once – I don't know – start – postcard

Unit 22

1 Do, does, don't oder doesn't?

A Where .... ¹ Mary live?
B In Oxford.
A .... ² she live near Ann?
B Yes, she .... ³.
A .... ⁴ her children live near her, too?
B Yes, they .... ⁵.

A .... ⁶ she see them every day?
B No, she .... ⁷. Not every day.
A .... ⁸ Mary and Ann meet very often?
B No, they .... ⁹. Not very often. Ann .... ¹⁰ have time.

2 Wer sind die unterstrichenen Personen? Sie sind Ihnen alle im Buch begegnet.

1 Bruno likes him a lot.
2 Ann knows her from Oxford. They are friends.
3 Her daughter-in-law doesn't get on very well with her.
4 They sometimes visit them in Boston.
5 She doesn't often visit them in Ebersberg.
6 Anke is married to him.

Unit 23
Was machen diese Personen gerade?

1 *He's writing a letter.*
2 She's .... radio.
3 They ....
4 She ....
5 He ....
6 He ....

Wörterverzeichnis nach Units

Unit 1
Übersetzung des Präsentationsdialogs

ANN Guten Tag, ich heiße Ann, Ann Thomas.
INGE Nett, Sie kennen zu lernen, Ann. Ich heiße Inge, Inge Schmitz.
ANN Nett, Sie kennen zu lernen.

ANN Woher sind/kommen Sie, Inge?
INGE Ich bin aus Deutschland.
ANN Und wo in Deutschland?
INGE Euskirchen. Das ist in der Nähe von Köln.

INGE Und Sie, Ann? Sind Sie aus England?
ANN Ja, das ist richtig.
INGE Und wo in England? Sind Sie aus London?
ANN Nein, ich bin nicht aus London. Ich bin aus Oxford.

1
hello	Hallo, guten Tag
my	mein/e
name	Name
is	ist
My name's (name is) …	Mein Name ist … / Ich heiße …
nice	nett, schön
to	zu
meet	kennen lernen; treffen; begegnen
you	du, ihr, Sie
Nice to meet you.	Nett, Sie kennen zu lernen.

2
where	wo, wohin
are	bist, seid, sind
from	von, her, aus
Where are you from?	Woher kommen/sind Sie?
I	ich
I'm (I am)	ich bin
Germany	Deutschland
and	und
in	in
that	das
near	in der Nähe von, nahe (bei)
Cologne	Köln
Austria	Österreich
Switzerland	die Schweiz
Munich	München
Berlin	Berlin
Vienna	Wien
Zurich	Zürich

3
Are you from …?	Sind Sie aus …?
England	England
yes	ja
right	richtig
Yes, that's right.	Ja, das ist richtig.
London	London
no	nein
not	nicht
No, I'm not.	Nein (bin ich nicht).
Oxford	Oxford
the	der, die, das
USA	USA
Australia	Australien
Canada	Kanada
France	Frankreich
Spain	Spanien
Italy	Italien
Britain	Großbritannien
United States	Vereinigte Staaten

Unit 2
Übersetzung des Präsentationsdialogs

INGE Ich habe eine Tochter in den USA, in der Nähe von Boston.
ANN Und ich habe einen Sohn in Deutschland!
INGE Wirklich?
ANN Ja.

ANN Er ist (lebt) in Bayern, in der Nähe von München.
INGE Ach ja.
ANN Seine Frau ist Deutsche. Und Ihre Tochter?
INGE Sie ist (lebt) in Boston. Ihr Mann ist Amerikaner.

ANN Kommen Sie und lernen Sie meine Freundin kennen. Sie ist dort drüben. Ihr Name ist Mary.

1
have	haben
a	ein/e
daughter	Tochter
son	Sohn
really	wirklich, tatsächlich
grandson	Enkelsohn
granddaughter	Enkeltochter
brother	Bruder
sister	Schwester
cousin	Cousin/e
godchild	Patenkind
nephew	Neffe

niece	Nichte
friend	Freund/in, Bekannte/r

2

he	er
he's (he is)	er ist
Bavaria	Bayern
oh	ach, oh (je)
his	sein/e
wife	Ehefrau
German	deutsch; Deutsch; Deutsch/e/r
your	dein/e, euer, eure, Ihr/e
she	sie
she's (she is)	sie ist
Boston	Boston
her	ihr/e
American	amerikanisch; Amerikanisch; Amerikaner/in
husband	Ehemann
girlfriend	Freundin
boyfriend	Freund
partner	Partner/in

3

come	kommen; kommen Sie
there	da, dort; dorthin
over there	da drüben

Unit 3
Übersetzung des Präsentationsdialogs

ANN	Mary, das ist Inge. Inge, das ist Mary.
INGE	Nett, Sie kennen zu lernen, Mary.
MARY	Guten Tag.
MARY	Entschuldigung. Wie ist Ihr Name?
INGE	Inge.
MARY	Inge. Ist das richtig?
INGE	Ja, das ist richtig.
INGE	Können/Sprechen Sie Deutsch, Ann?
ANN	Ja (kann ich). Ein wenig.
INGE	Ach gut!

1

this	dies, das; diese/r/s

2

Excuse me …	Entschuldigen Sie …
me	mich
what	was
What's your name?	Wie heißen Sie?
it	es
first name	Vorname
surname	Familienname
address	Adresse
of	von
town	Stadt
street	Straße

3

can	können
speak	sprechen
a little	ein wenig, ein bisschen
good	gut
English	englisch; Englisch
French	französisch; Französisch
Italian	italienisch; Italienisch
Spanish	spanisch; Spanisch
I'm afraid not.	Leider nicht.

Unit 4
Übersetzung des Präsentationsdialogs

INGE	Ich bin mit meinem Mann hier. Wir sind mit seinem Verein hier. Wie heißt „Bowlingverein" auf Englisch, Ann?
ANN	…
INGE	Nun, wir sind mit dem Bowlingverein meines Mannes hier.
ANN	Meine Schwiegertochter ist Mitglied in einem Bowlingverein.
INGE	Ach wirklich!
MARY	Wie heißt Ihr Mann, Inge?
INGE	Bruno.
INGE	Bruno ist da drüben mit seinen Freunden. Sie sind alle in der Bar. Ich muss jetzt gehen.
ANN	Okay. Bis später.
INGE	Ja, auf Wiedersehen.
MARY	Wiedersehen, Inge.

1

here	hier
with	mit
we	wir
we're (we are)	wir sind
club	Klub, Verein
What's … in English?	Wie heißt … auf Englisch?
bowling club	Bowlingverein
sports club	Sportverein
hiking club	Wanderverein
tour group	Reisegruppe
church	Kirche
choir	Chor
English class	Englischkurs
twin town	Partnerstadt

2

well	nun
my husband's bowling club	der Bowlingverein meines Mannes
daughter-in-law	Schwiegertochter
member	Mitglied
a member of a club	Mitglied in einem Verein
neighbour	Nachbar/in

best	beste/r/s
teacher	Lehrer/in
son-in-law	Schwiegersohn

3

they	sie
they're (they are)	sie sind
all	all/e
bar	Bar
must	müssen
go	gehen; fahren
now	jetzt, nun
OK	OK, okay, in Ordnung
See you later.	Bis später.
goodbye	auf Wiedersehen
bye-bye	Wiedersehen, Tschüss
hotel	Hotel
coach	(Reise-)Bus
restaurant	Restaurant
museum	Museum

Unit 6
Übersetzung des Präsentationsdialogs

ANN Guten Morgen, Inge. Wie geht es Ihnen heute?
INGE Gut, danke.
ANN Und Ihnen, Bruno? Wie geht es Ihnen?
BRUNO Ach, OK. Zu viel Bier gestern Abend, leider.

ANN Möchten Sie etwas Kaffee?
INGE Ja gerne.
ANN Und Sie Bruno? Möchten Sie etwas Kaffee?
BRUNO Nein danke.
ANN Möchten Sie etwas Tee? Oder Wasser?
BRUNO Wasser bitte.

INGE Wo ist Mary?
ANN In unserer Kabine.
INGE Ach. Ist alles in Ordnung mit ihr?
ANN Nein, leider nicht. Es geht ihr heute Morgen nicht gut.
INGE Ach, das tut mir Leid.

1

Good morning.	Guten Morgen.
today	heute
how	wie
How are you?	Wie geht es dir/euch/ Ihnen?
Fine, thanks.	Gut, danke.
too much beer	zu viel Bier
last night	letzte Nacht; gestern Abend
Good afternoon.	Guten Tag. (nachmittags)
Good evening.	Guten Abend.
Not so bad.	Geht so.

so	so
very	sehr
I'm not very well.	Mir geht es nicht (sehr) gut.

2

Would you like …?	Möchtest du / Möchtet ihr / Möchten Sie …?
some	etwas
coffee	Kaffee
please	bitte
Yes, please.	Ja bitte. / Ja gerne.
No, thank you.	Nein danke.
tea	Tee
or	oder
water	Wasser
wine	Wein
juice	Saft
milk	Milch

3

our	unser/e
cabin	Kabine
No, she isn't.	Nein (ist sie nicht).
I'm sorry.	Es/Das tut mir Leid.

Unit 7
Übersetzung des Präsentationsdialogs

BRUNO Kann ich bitte die Butter haben?
ANN Ja natürlich. Bitte (sehr/schön).
BRUNO Danke schön.
ANN Bitte. / Keine Ursache.

ANN Sagen Sie mal. Wer ist der Mann da drüben? Ist er in Ihrem Bowlingverein?
BRUNO Nein (ist er nicht).
INGE Er ist sehr müde.
ANN Ja (ist er).

ANN Und die Leute da drüben – sind sie in Ihrem Verein?
BRUNO Ja (sind sie).
INGE Ihre Kabine ist neben unserer Kabine.
Ihr Name ist Mayer.
ANN Sind sie verheiratet?
INGE Nein (sind sie nicht). Sie sind beide unverheiratet. Sie sind Geschwister, Rolf und Trudi Mayer.

1

butter	Butter
of course	natürlich
Here you are.	Bitte schön/sehr.
You're welcome.	Keine Ursache. / Bitte sehr.
sugar	Zucker
salt	Salz
pepper	Pfeffer
bread	Brot

2

Tell me.	Sagen Sie mal.
who	wer
man	Mann
No, he isn't.	Nein (ist er nicht).
tired	müde
tall	groß (gewachsen)
short	kurz (gewachsen)
athletic	sportlich
good-looking	gut aussehend
fat	dick
slim	schlank
old	alt
young	jung

3

people	Leute, Personen
Yes, they are.	Ja (sind sie).
their	ihr/e
next to	neben
married	verheiratet
No, they aren't.	Nein (sind sie nicht).
both	beide
single	allein stehend, ledig

Unit 8

Übersetzung des Präsentationsdialogs

ANN: Wie viele Personen gibt es in Brunos Verein?
INGE: Lassen Sie mal sehen. Es gibt eins, zwei, drei, vier, fünf Ehepaare. Das sind zehn Leute. Die Mayers, zwölf. Franz und Willi Günther, vierzehn. Und Irmgard und Ulla, sechzehn.
ANN: Sechzehn Personen insgesamt?
INGE: Ja, sechzehn, mit Ehepartnern und Freunden. Acht Männer und acht Frauen.
ANN: Ihr Englisch ist sehr gut, Inge.
INGE: Es ist nett von Ihnen, das zu sagen. Danke. Bruno und ich sind Mitglieder in einem Englischkurs.
ANN: Ist das ein Abendkurs?
INGE: Ja, das ist richtig. Unser Lehrer ist Engländer.
ANN: Oh.

How many … are there?	Wie viele … gibt es?

1

Let me see.	Lassen Sie/Lass(t) mal sehen.
there are	es gibt/sind
one	eins
two	zwei
three	drei
four	vier
five	fünf
couple	Ehepaar
That's ten people.	Das sind zehn Leute.
twelve	zwölf
fourteen	vierzehn
sixteen	sechzehn
altogether	insgesamt
wives	Ehefrauen
eight	acht
men	Männer
woman, women	Frau, Frauen

2

That's nice of you.	Das ist nett von Ihnen.
say	sagen
That's nice of you to say so.	Es ist nett von Ihnen, das zu sagen.
an (vor a, e, i, o, u, wenn das u wie a gesprochen wird)	ein/e
class	Kurs, Klasse
Englishman	Engländer
Englishwoman	Engländerin
accent	Akzent
pronunciation	Aussprache
pullover	Pullover
watch	(Armband-)Uhr
blouse	Bluse
dress	Kleid

Unit 9

Übersetzung des Präsentationsdialogs

ANN: Wo in Deutschland kommen Sie her?
INGE: Wir leben in Euskirchen. Das liegt südwestlich von Köln.
BRUNO: Es ist eine mittelgroße Stadt.
INGE: Und Ihr Sohn, Ann?
ANN: Er lebt im Süden von Deutschland. In Ebersberg.
BRUNO: Ach ja. Das ist nicht weit von München.
ANN: Das ist richtig. Es liegt etwa 30 Kilometer östlich von München.
BRUNO: Wir sind ursprünglich nicht aus Euskirchen. Ich bin ursprünglich aus Magdeburg.
ANN: Und Sie, Inge?
INGE: Ich bin nicht aus Ostdeutschland. Ich bin ursprünglich aus Mannheim.

1

live	wohnen, leben
south-west of	südwestlich von
medium-sized	mittelgroß
north of	nördlich von
south of	südlich von
east of	östlich von

west of	westlich von	**1**	
place	Ort, Platz, Stelle	about	über, von
city	Großstadt	Tell me about …	Erzählen Sie mir von …
village	Dorf	tell	erzählen
big	groß	What is there …?	Was gibt es (dort) …?
small	klein	to do	zu tun
		there's (there is)	es gibt
2		there isn't	es gibt kein/e
he lives	er wohnt/lebt	theatre	Theater
in the south of Germany	im Süden von Deutschland	but	aber
far	weit	really	eigentlich
about	etwa	interesting	interessant
thirty	dreißig	carnival	Karneval
kilometre	Kilometer	too	auch
in the north of	im Norden von	football team	Fußballmannschaft
in the east of	im Osten von	football	Fußball
in the west of	im Westen von	park	Park(anlage)
in the middle of	in der Mitte von	beautiful	schön, herrlich
forty	vierzig	countryside	Landschaft
fifty	fünfzig	river	Fluss
sixty	sechzig	new	neu
seventy	siebzig	swimming pool	Schwimmbad
eighty	achtzig	modern	modern
ninety	neunzig	sports centre	Sportzentrum
a/one hundred	(ein)hundert	cinema	Kino
		famous	berühmt, bedeutend
3		castle	Burg; Schloss
we aren't	wir sind nicht		
originally	ursprünglich	**2**	
East Germany	Ostdeutschland	What else?	Was sonst?; Was noch?
		some	einige, ein paar

Unit 11
Übersetzung des Präsentationsdialogs

ANN	Erzählen Sie mir von Euskirchen. Was gibt es dort zu tun und zu sehen?
INGE	Es gibt ein schönes Theater. Aber es gibt eigentlich kein interessantes Museum.
BRUNO	Es gibt einen guten Bowlingverein! Und es gibt auch den Karneval. Aber es gibt keine gute Fußballmannschaft.
INGE	Es gibt eigentlich keinen großen Park. Aber die Landschaft in der Nähe von Euskirchen ist schön. Die Eifel.
ANN	Ach ja. Die Eifel.
ANN	Was gibt es (sonst) noch?
INGE	Es gibt einige nette Orte in der Nähe von Euskirchen.
BRUNO	Es gibt einige gute Kneipen.
INGE	Es gibt nicht viele gute Geschäfte. Aber wir sind nicht weit von Köln und Bonn entfernt.
BRUNO	Es gibt keine guten Nachtlokale.
INGE	Ach Bruno!

pub	Pub, Kneipe, Gaststätte
a lot of	viel/e
shop	Geschäft, Laden
There aren't any …	Es gibt keine …
night club	Nachtclub
building	Gebäude
house	Haus

Unit 12
Übersetzung des Präsentationsdialogs

BRUNO	Erzählen Sie mir von Oxford. Gibt es eine gute Fußballmannschaft?
MARY	Nein (gibt es nicht). Tut mir Leid, Bruno.
ANN	Es gibt einen Fußballverein, aber er ist nicht sehr gut.
BRUNO	Gibt es Karneval?
ANN	Ja (gibt es). Aber es ist nicht wie der deutsche Karneval.
BRUNO	Gibt es gute Pubs?
MARY	Ja (gibt es).
BRUNO	Gibt es viele Nachtclubs?
ANN	Nein (gibt es nicht). Tut mir Leid, Bruno.
INGE	Oxford ist eine alte Universitätsstadt.
BRUNO	Ja, ich weiß, aber …

ANN	Möchten Sie (einige) Fotos sehen?
INGE	Ja gerne.
MARY	Dies ist eines der alten Colleges.
INGE	Ach schön.

1
No, there isn't.	Nein (gibt es nicht).
sorry	tut mir Leid
football club	Fußballverein
like	wie

2
an old university town	eine alte Universitätsstadt
I know	ich weiß

3
Would you like to see …?	Möchten Sie … sehen?
photo	Foto
college	Institut; College
lovely	schön, herrlich
perhaps	vielleicht, eventuell
can't	kann nicht
just now	gerade, im Moment
go for a meal	essen gehen
meal	Mahlzeit, Essen
go for a drink	etwas trinken gehen
drink	Getränk
go to the theatre	ins Theater gehen
go to the cinema	ins Kino gehen
go shopping	einkaufen gehen
shopping	Einkaufen
visit	besuchen
family	Familie

Unit 13
Übersetzung des Präsentationsdialogs

INGE	Mary, erzählen Sie mir von Ihrer Familie.
MARY	Nun, ich habe einen Sohn, John. Er ist verheiratet und hat zwei Töchter.
INGE	Ach schön.
MARY	Ich habe auch eine Tochter. Sie ist geschieden. Sie hat zwei Jungen.
INGE	Also haben Sie vier Enkelkinder.
MARY	Ja, das ist richtig.
INGE	Wie alt sind Ihre Enkelkinder?
MARY	Die zwei Jungen, Craig und Alexander, sind zwölf und neun. Und meine Enkeltöchter sind fünf und drei.
INGE	Ach schön.
MARY	Die Kinder haben auch Tiere. Craig und Alexander haben einen Hund. Und die Familie meines Sohnes hat eine Katze namens Samson.
INGE	Das ist ein lustiger Name für eine Katze.
INGE	Dieser Kaffee ist kalt.
MARY	Oh je!
INGE	Ist Ihr Tee okay?
MARY	Ja, er ist gut so.
INGE	Gut!

1
he has	er hat
also	auch
divorced	geschieden
boy	Junge
so	also
grandchildren	Enkelkinder
child, children	Kind, Kinder
no	kein/e
relative	Verwandte/r
girl	Mädchen

2
animal	Tier
dog	Hund
cat	Katze
called	namens, genannt
funny	lustig, komisch
for	für

3
cold	kalt
Oh dear!	Oh je! Oh schade!
fine	gut (so); (ganz) in Ordnung
Oh good!	Gut! Prima!
hot	heiß; warm
warm	warm
awful	schrecklich
noisy	laut
late	(zu) spät, verspätet

Unit 14
Übersetzung des Präsentationsdialogs

ANN	Entschuldigen Sie, wie spät ist es bitte?
MAN	Es ist 10 Uhr.
ANN	Und wann werden wir in Tanger sein?
MAN	In einer Stunde, um 11 Uhr.
ANN	Und wann wird das Schiff wieder abfahren?
MAN	Um halb acht.
ANN	Also wie viel Zeit werden wir dort haben?
MAN	Achteinhalb Stunden.
ANN	Um wie viel Uhr wird (das) Abendessen heute abend sein?

MAN	Um acht Uhr anstatt halb acht. Es wird eine Ansage in 15 Minuten geben, um Viertel nach zehn. Die nächste Ansage wird um Viertel vor elf sein.	INGE	Wie ist es mit Ihrer Freizeit?
		ANN	Nun, am Abend sehe ich oft fern oder lese. Aber am Dienstag gehe ich immer zu einem Gymnastikkurs.
		INGE	Und ich gehe immer zu meinem Englischkurs.
		ANN	Am Dienstag?
		INGE	Ja, und am Donnerstag treffe ich mich oft mit Freund(inn)en.
		ANN	Manchmal esse ich am Sonntag mit Freund(inn)en zu Mittag.

What time is it? Wie spät ist es?
time Zeit

1

It's 10 o'clock. Es ist 10 Uhr.
when wann
will werden
Tangier Tanger
hour Stunde
at 11 o'clock um 11 Uhr
What is the time? Wie spät ist es?

2

ship Schiff
leave (ab)fahren; verlassen
again wieder; noch einmal
half past seven halb acht
eight and a half achteinhalb
half halb; Hälfte
arrive ankommen
plane Flugzeug
train Zug, Eisenbahn

3

dinner (festliches) Abendessen
this evening heute Abend
instead of anstatt; anstelle von
There will be … Es wird … geben.
announcement Ansage, Ankündigung
minute Minute
quarter past ten Viertel nach zehn
next nächste/r/s
quarter to eleven Viertel vor elf
breakfast Frühstück
lunch Mittagessen
tea Teezeit

Unit 16
Übersetzung des Präsentationsdialogs

ANN	Es ist schön, spät aufzustehen. Ich stehe normalerweise um sieben Uhr auf. Wie ist es mit Ihnen?
INGE	Ich stehe normalerweise um sechs auf. Ich fange um halb acht an zu arbeiten.
ANN	Das ist früh.
INGE	Ich arbeite am Montag, Dienstag und Donnerstag.
ANN	Ach, Sie arbeiten Teilzeit.
INGE	Ja, das ist richtig. Wie ist es mit Ihnen?
ANN	Ich arbeite Vollzeit.

get up aufstehen

1

usually normalerweise, gewöhnlich
What about you? Was ist mit Ihnen?, Wie ist es mit Ihnen?
work Arbeit; arbeiten
start work anfangen zu arbeiten
early früh
have breakfast frühstücken
have lunch zu Mittag essen
have dinner/supper zu Abend essen
finish work aufhören zu arbeiten
finish aufhören
go to bed ins Bett gehen

2

on Monday am Montag, montags
Tuesday Dienstag
Thursday Donnerstag
part-time Teilzeit
full-time Vollzeit, ganztags
full voll
housewife Hausfrau
I'm a housewife. Ich bin Hausfrau.
retired im Ruhestand, pensioniert
I'm retired. Ich bin im Ruhestand.
Wednesday Mittwoch
Friday Freitag
Saturday Samstag, Sonnabend
Sunday Sonntag

3

free time Freizeit
in the evening am Abend, abends
often oft, meistens
watch TV fernsehen
TV Fernsehen
read lesen
always immer
go to a class einen Kurs besuchen
gymnastics Gymnastik
sometimes manchmal
never nie
listen to music Musik hören
listen to the radio Radio hören
garden Garten

Unit 17
Übersetzung des Präsentationsdialogs

ANN   Ich frühstücke meistens nicht viel. Ich habe normalerweise keine Zeit, wenn ich zu Hause bin. Wie ist es mit Ihnen?

INGE   Ich esse nicht viel zu Mittag. Aber ich frühstücke immer gut. Ich fange um halb acht an zu arbeiten. Aber ich habe immer Zeit.

ANN   Sie stehen um sechs auf, richtig?

INGE   Ja. So beginne ich immer den Tag. Auf um sechs, zwanzig Minuten für das Frühstück mit schönem heißen Kaffee, Brot, Käse und Wurst – und dann gehe ich zur Arbeit.

ANN   In Großbritannien essen wir normalerweise keinen Käse und keinen Aufschnitt zum Frühstück.

INGE   Und die Leute trinken keinen Kaffee, nur Tee. Ist das richtig?

ANN   Nun, einige Leute trinken Tee, einige trinken Kaffee. Aber es ist oft Pulverkaffee.

INGE   Wie ist es mit dem Abendessen?

ANN   Nun, das Abendessen ist oft eine warme Mahlzeit.

INGE   Sie meinen, die Leute essen nicht Brot und Käse und Wurst?

ANN   Normalerweise nicht.

INGE   Das ist unser normales Abendessen. Und Bruno trinkt eine Flasche Bier.

ANN   Die Leute trinken normalerweise kein Bier zum Abendessen in Großbritannien. Ich mag Bier nicht besonders. Aber ich mag Wein.

I don't eat	ich esse nicht

1

when	wenn
at home	zu Hause
have a big lunch	viel zu Mittag essen
have a good breakfast	gut/reichhaltig frühstücken
day	Tag
up	auf, hoch
cheese	Käse
sausage	Wurst

2

for breakfast	zum Frühstück
drink	trinken
only	nur
have tea	Tee trinken
instant coffee	Pulverkaffee, löslicher Kaffee
roll	Brötchen
jam	Marmelade
cornflakes	Cornflakes
fruit	Obst
ham	Schinken
bacon and eggs	Speck und Eier
egg	Ei
muesli	Müsli
fish	Fisch

3

You mean …	Sie meinen / wollen sagen …
have bread	Brot essen
normal	normal, gewöhnlich, üblich
a bottle of beer	eine Flasche Bier
with their supper	zum Abendessen
I don't like beer much.	Ich mag Bier nicht besonders. / Ich trinke Bier nicht besonders gern.
like	mögen, gern (essen, trinken)

Unit 18
Übersetzung des Präsentationsdialogs

INGE   Erzählen Sie mir von Ihrem Sohn.

ANN   Nun, er wohnt in Ebersberg und arbeitet in München. Er arbeitet viel. Aber am Wochenende macht er viel Sport. Im Sommer geht er auf dem Chiemsee windsurfen. Im Herbst geht er in den Bergen wandern. Und im Winter und im Frühling geht er Ski fahren. Seine Frau mag Musik. Sie singt in einem Chor. Manchmal gehen sie zu Konzerten in München.

INGE   In Bayern kann man gut leben.

ANN   Und Euskirchen?

INGE   Nun, man kann in der Eifel wandern oder manchmal Ski fahren. Aber Euskirchen ist nicht München.

ANN   Was ist ein typischer Sonntag für Sie?

INGE   Nun, im Winter ist der Sonntag ruhig. Ich stehe spät auf und frühstücke mit Bruno. Dann lese ich die Wochenendzeitung. Ich gehe in die Kirche. Dann koche ich das Mittagessen und manchmal backe ich einen Kuchen. Nach dem Mittagessen gehe ich oft mit Bruno und dem Hund spazieren. Dann telefoniere ich oder schreibe einen Brief oder eine E-Mail an meine Tochter. Am Abend sehen wir oft fern. Aber im Sommer ist es anders.

1

a lot	viel; sehr
at the weekend	am Wochenende
he does sport	er macht/treibt Sport
summer	Sommer
go windsurfing	windsurfen gehen
autumn	Herbst
go hiking	wandern gehen
mountain	Berg
winter	Winter
spring	Frühling
go skiing	Ski fahren gehen
concert	Konzert
Bavaria is a nice place to live.	In Bayern kann man gut leben.

2

You can go hiking.	Man kann wandern gehen.
typical	typisch
quiet	ruhig
then	dann
newspaper	Zeitung
go to church	in die Kirche gehen
cook	kochen
make a cake	einen Kuchen backen
make	machen, anfertigen, herstellen
cake	Kuchen
after	nach
after lunch	nach dem Mittagessen
go for a walk	spazieren gehen, einen Spaziergang machen
phone	telefonieren
write	schreiben
letter	Brief
email	E-Mail
to my daughter	an meine Tochter
different	anders

Unit 19
Übersetzung des Präsentationsdialogs

ANN Das Schiff macht morgen in Madeira Halt.
INGE Ja. Es ist schön dort.
ANN Ach, Sie kennen es?
INGE Ja. Jedes Jahr im Winter machen wir Urlaub in der Sonne. Bruno mag den Winter nicht. Er mag die Kälte nicht. Er mag den Sommer am liebsten.
ANN Mir macht die Kälte nichts aus. Aber ich mag die Hitze nicht.

ANN Wie ist das Klima in Madeira?
INGE Es wird nicht zu heiß. Es wird nicht zu kalt. Es schneit nicht.
ANN Wie ist es mit Regen?
INGE Es regnet. Aber es regnet nicht zu viel. Es ist schön warm.

ANN Was sollen wir in Funchal tun?
INGE Nun, es gibt einen sehr schönen Markt. Sollen wir dorthin gehen?
ANN Ja, das ist eine nette Idee.
INGE Und sollen wir die Kathedrale besuchen?
ANN Lieber nicht.
INGE Okay, lassen Sie uns zum Markt gehen.
ANN Wir können Reiseandenken kaufen.
INGE Bruno will etwas Madeirawein kaufen.

What's the weather like?	Wie ist das Wetter?
weather	Wetter

1

stop	anhalten, Halt machen, stoppen; aufhören
tomorrow	morgen
know	kennen
every	jede/r/s
year	Jahr
have a holiday	(einen) Urlaub machen
holiday	Urlaub
sun	Sonne
doesn't like	mag nicht
cold	Kälte
like best	am liebsten haben/mögen
I don't mind the cold.	Mir macht (die) Kälte nichts aus. / Ich habe nichts gegen (die) Kälte.
heat	Hitze

2

climate	Klima
it doesn't get	es wird nicht
get	werden
it doesn't snow	es schneit nicht
snow	schneien
rain	Regen; regnen
it doesn't rain	es regnet nicht
nice and warm	schön warm

3

shall	sollen
market	Markt
idea	Idee
cathedral	Kathedrale, Dom
I'd rather not	(ich würde) lieber nicht
Let's ...	Lassen Sie uns / Lass(t) uns ...
buy	kaufen
souvenir	Reiseandenken, Souvenir
want to	wollen
Bruno wants to buy ...	Bruno will ... kaufen

Unit 21
Übersetzung des Präsentationsdialogs

INGE	Postkarten für Ihre Familie, Mary?
MARY	Ja. Eine für meine Enkelsöhne, eine für meine Enkeltöchter.
INGE	Sehen Sie Ihre Familie oft?
MARY	Ja (tue ich). Sie wohnen alle in der Nähe.
INGE	Das ist schön.
MARY	Sehen Sie und Bruno Ihre Tochter oft?
INGE	Nein (tun wir nicht), leider. Etwa einmal im Jahr. Boston ist so weit weg.
INGE	Kennen Sie Boston, Ann? Oder Neuengland?
ANN	Nein (tue ich nicht). Ich kenne Teile der Westküste ziemlich gut. Kennen Sie Kalifornien?
INGE	Nicht sehr gut. Wo ist der Ladenbesitzer nun?
ANN	Was meinen Sie? Sprechen sie hier Englisch?
INGE	Ja (tun sie). Ich bin sicher. Nun, ich bin sicher, dass sie es verstehen. Ist das der Ladenbesitzer?
ANN	Ich weiß (es) nicht. Kommen Sie, wir fragen.

Do they speak English?	Sprechen sie Englisch?

1

postcard	Postkarte
Do you often see …?	Sehen Sie … oft?
Yes, I do.	Ja (tue ich).; Doch!
nearby	in der Nähe, nahebei
No, we don't.	Nein (tun wir nicht).
once a year	einmal im Jahr
once	einmal, ein Mal
far away	weit weg
away	weg
twice	zweimal
week	Woche
three times	dreimal, drei Mal
month	Monat

2

Do you know …?	Kennen Sie / Kennst du …?
New England	Neuengland
No, I don't.	Nein (tue ich nicht).
part	Teil
coast	Küste
California	Kalifornien
quite	ziemlich
well	gut
Not very well.	Nicht sehr gut.
shopkeeper	Ladenbesitzer/in

3

think	meinen, glauben
Yes, they do.	Ja (tun sie).
I'm sure	ich bin (mir) sicher
understand	verstehen
I'm sure they understand it.	Ich bin (mir) sicher, dass sie es verstehen.
I don't know.	Ich weiß (es) nicht.
ask	fragen; befragen

Unit 22
Übersetzung des Präsentationsdialogs

INGE	Sind dies Ihr Sohn und seine Frau?
ANN	Ja.
INGE	Vermisst er England?
ANN	Nein (tut er nicht). Es gefällt ihm in Bayern.
INGE	Spricht seine Frau Englisch?
ANN	Ja (tut sie). Aber leider kommen wir nicht gut miteinander aus.
INGE	Oh je, das tut mir Leid. Macht das die Dinge sehr schwierig, wenn Sie sie sehen?
ANN	Ja (tut es), leider. Und Sie? Verstehen Sie und Bruno sich mit Ihrem Schwiegersohn?
INGE	Ja (tun wir). Wir haben viel Glück. Bruno mag Glenn sehr.
ANN	Spricht Glenn Deutsch?
INGE	Nein (tut er nicht).
ANN	Nun, Sie und Bruno sprechen Englisch, also ist das kein Problem. Vermisst Ihre Tochter Deutschland?
INGE	Nein (tut sie nicht). Aber ich vermisse sie manchmal. Sie ist sehr glücklich in Amerika. Sie will dort bleiben.
INGE	Schauen Sie. Dies ist ein Foto von ihr.
ANN	Oh, ist sie nicht hübsch?
INGE	Und dies ist Glenn. Sehen Sie sich ihn an. Ich mag ihn mit dem Hut.
ANN	Ja. Ist es nicht schön?
INGE	Dies ist ein Foto von uns in … Ach, ich kann mich jetzt nicht an den Namen des Ortes erinnern. Ich muss sie fragen, wenn ich sie wiedersehe.

Does she speak English?	Spricht sie Englisch?

1

Does he miss England?	Vermisst er England?
miss	vermissen
No, he doesn't.	Nein (tut er nicht).

Does his wife speak English?	Spricht seine Frau Englisch?
Yes, she does.	Ja (tut sie).
We don't get on very well.	Wir kommen nicht gut miteinander aus.
Does that make things difficult?	Macht das die Dinge schwierig?
thing	Ding, Sache
difficult	schwierig
them	sie
Yes, it does.	Ja (tut es).
Yes, we do.	Ja (tun wir).
We're lucky.	Wir haben Glück.
Bruno likes Glenn a lot.	Bruno mag Glenn sehr.
problem	Problem
No, she doesn't.	Nein (tut sie nicht).
her	sie, ihr
happy	glücklich
stay	bleiben; übernachten

2

Look!	Schauen Sie!
photo of her	Foto von ihr
Isn't she pretty?	Ist sie nicht hübsch?
pretty	hübsch
Look at him.	Sehen/Schauen Sie ihn an.
him	ihn, ihm
in that hat	mit dem Hut
that	jene/r/s (dort); diese/r/s (hier)
hat	Hut
of us	von uns
us	uns
remember	sich erinnern (an)
jacket	Jacke, Jackett
skirt	Rock
shirt	Hemd
pair of trousers	Hose
smart	schick
unusual	ungewöhnlich

Unit 23
Übersetzung des Präsentationsdialogs

MARY	Entschuldigen Sie. Gehören Sie zu dem deutschen Bowlingverein?
MANN	Nein, leider nicht.
MARY	Ach, Entschuldigung.
MANN	Keine Ursache.
MARY	Entschuldigen Sie. Gehören Sie zu dem deutschen Bowlingverein?
MANN	Ja.
MARY	Ach gut. Können Sie mir bitte helfen? Ich suche Inge und Brunos Kabine. Wissen Sie, welche Nummer das ist?
MANN	Ja, es ist Kabine Nummer 337.
MARY	Danke.
MANN	Sie packen im Moment. Das heißt, Inge packt und Bruno hilft. Er trinkt (gerade) die letzte Flasche Madeirawein aus und singt ihr etwas vor.
MARY	Ach!

I'm sorry.	Entschuldigung.
That's all right.	Das ist in Ordnung. / Macht nichts. / Keine Ursache. / Schon gut.

2

help	helfen
I'm looking for	ich suche (gerade)
which	welche/r/s
number	Nummer, Zahl, Ziffer
they're packing	sie packen (gerade)
pack	packen
at the moment	im Moment, im Augenblick
moment	Moment, Augenblick
or rather	das heißt, oder eigentlich
he's finishing …	er trinkt (gerade) … aus
the last bottle of Madeira wine	die letzte Flasche Madeirawein
he's singing to her	er singt ihr (gerade) etwas vor
sing	singen
room	Zimmer, Raum

Unit 24
Übersetzung des Präsentationsdialogs

ANN	Inge, kann ich Ihre Adresse haben?
INGE	Sie lautet „In den Hüppen 26, 53879 Euskirchen".
ANN	Können Sie den Namen der Straße bitte buchstabieren?
INGE	Natürlich. Er lautet „In", neues Wort „den", D E N, neues Wort „Hüppen", H U-Umlaut, Doppel-P E N.
ANN	In den Hüppen. Das ist ein komischer Name.
INGE	Ja (ist er). Ich muss ihn auch oft für Deutsche buchstabieren.
ANN	Und wie lautet noch mal die Postleitzahl für Euskirchen?
INGE	53879.
ANN	53879. Gut, danke.
ANN	Und wie ist Ihre Telefonnummer bitte?
INGE	Sie lautet 02251 – das ist die Vorwahl – und die Nummer ist 34529.
ANN	02251-34529. Gut.
INGE	Und wie ist Ihre Adresse und Telefonnummer, Ann?
ANN	Hier sind sie – auf diesem Blatt Papier.
INGE	Danke.

INGE	Nun, es ist Zeit, auf Wiedersehen zu sagen. Auf Wiedersehen, Mary. Es war sehr schön, Sie kennen zu lernen.
MARY	Auf Wiedersehen, Inge.
INGE	Wenn Sie Ihren Sohn besuchen, Ann, müssen Sie uns für ein paar Tage besuchen kommen.
ANN	Ich würde Sie sehr gern wiedersehen. Sie und Bruno müssen in England Urlaub machen. Im Sommer, Bruno, wenn es warm ist.
BRUNO	Nun, wir wollen nächstes Jahr Anke in Boston besuchen. Vielleicht werden wir über London fliegen.

1

Can you spell …?	Können Sie … buchstabieren?
spell	buchstabieren
word	Wort
double	Doppel-, doppelt
I often have to spell it.	Ich muss ihn oft buchstabieren.
have to	müssen
German people	Deutsche
postcode	Postleitzahl

2

What's your telephone number?	Wie ist Ihre Telefonnummer?
telephone	Telefon
code	Vorwahl(nummer)
phone number = telephone number	
piece of paper	Blatt Papier
piece	Blatt, Stück
paper	Papier

3

It was lovely to meet you.	Es war sehr schön, Sie kennen zu lernen.
You must come and visit us.	Sie müssen uns besuchen kommen.
visit	besuchen
for a few days	ein paar Tage (lang)
a few	ein paar
I'd love to …	Ich würde sehr gern …
fly	fliegen
via	über

Wörterverzeichnis alphabetisch

a

a [ə, eɪ] ein/e *2*; **a few** ein paar *24*; **a little** ein wenig, ein bisschen *3*; **a lot** viel; sehr *18*; **a lot of** viel/e *11*
about [əˈbaʊt] etwa *9*; über, von *11*
accent [ˈæksent] Akzent *8*
address [əˈdres] Adresse *3*
afraid [əˈfreɪd]; **I'm afraid (not).** Leider (nicht). *3*
after [ˈɑːftə] nach *18*
afternoon [ˌɑːftəˈnuːn] Nachmittag *6*; **Good afternoon.** Guten Tag. (nachmittags) *6*; **in the afternoon** nachmittags *14*
again [əˈgen] wieder; noch einmal *14*
all [ɔːl] all/e *4*; **all right** in Ordnung *23*; **That's all right.** Macht nichts. / Keine Ursache. *23*
also [ˈɔːlsəʊ] auch *13*
altogether [ˌɔːltəˈgeðə] insgesamt *8*
always [ˈɔːlweɪz] immer *16*
am [æm] bin *1*
am [ˌeɪ ˈem] (ante meridiem) vormittags *14*
American [əˈmerɪkən] amerikanisch; Amerikanisch; Amerikaner/in *2*
an [ən] ein/e *8*
and [ənd] und *1*
animal [ˈænɪml] Tier *13*
announcement [əˈnaʊnsmənt] Ansage, Ankündigung *14*
any [ˈeni]; **not any** kein/e *11*
are [ɑː] bist, seid, sind *1*; **aren't** sind nicht *9*
arrive [əˈraɪv] ankommen *14*
ask [ɑːsk] fragen; befragen *21*
at [æt]; **at 11 o'clock** um 11 Uhr *14*; **at home** zu Hause *17*; **at the moment** im Moment/Augenblick *23*; **at the weekend** am Wochenende *18*; **Look at him.** Schauen/Sehen Sie ihn an. *22*
athletic [æθˈletɪk] sportlich *7*
Australia [ɒˈstreɪliə] Australien *1*
Austria [ˈɒstriə] Österreich *1*
autumn [ˈɔːtəm] Herbst *18*
away [əˈweɪ] weg *21*
awful [ˈɔːfl] schrecklich *13*

b

bacon and eggs [ˌbeɪkən ənd ˈegz] Speck und Eier *17*
bad [bæd] schlecht *6*; **Not so bad.** Geht so. *6*
bar [bɑː] Bar *4*
Bavaria [bəˈveəriə] Bayern *2*
be [biː] sein *4*; **be lucky** Glück haben *22*
beautiful [ˈbjuːtɪfl] schön, herrlich *11*
bed [bed] Bett *16*; **go to bed** ins Bett gehen *16*
beer [bɪə] Bier *6*
Berlin [bɜːˈlɪn] Berlin *1*
best [best] beste/r/s *4*; **like best** am liebsten haben/mögen *19*
big [bɪg] groß *9*; **have a big lunch/breakfast** viel zu Mittag essen/frühstücken *17*
blouse [blaʊz] Bluse *8*
Boston [ˈbɒstn] Boston *2*
both [bəʊθ] beide *7*
bottle [ˈbɒtl] Flasche *17*; **a bottle of beer** eine Flasche Bier *17*
bowling club [ˈbəʊlɪŋ ˌklʌb] Bowlingverein *4*
boy [bɔɪ] Junge *13*
boyfriend [ˈbɔɪfrend] Freund *2*
bread [bred] Brot *7*
breakfast [ˈbrekfəst] Frühstück *14*; **have breakfast** frühstücken *16*
Britain [ˈbrɪtn] Großbritannien *1*
brother [ˈbrʌðə] Bruder *2*
building [ˈbɪldɪŋ] Gebäude *11*
but [bʌt] aber *11*
butter [ˈbʌtə] Butter *7*
buy [baɪ] kaufen *19*
bye-bye [ˌbaɪˈbaɪ] Wiedersehen, Tschüss *4*

c

cabin [ˈkæbɪn] Kabine *6*
cake [keɪk] Kuchen *18*; **make a cake** einen Kuchen backen *18*
California [kæləˈfɔːniə] Kalifornien *21*
called [kɔːld] namens, genannt *13*
can [kæn] können *3*
can't [kɑːnt] Verneinung von can *12*
Canada [ˈkænədə] Kanada *1*
carnival [ˈkɑːnɪvl] Karneval *11*
castle [ˈkɑːsl] Burg; Schloss *11*
cat [kæt] Katze *13*
cathedral [kəˈθiːdrəl] Kathedrale, Dom *19*
cheese [tʃiːz] Käse *17*
child [tʃaɪld] Kind *13*
children [ˈtʃɪldrən] Kinder *13*
choir [ˈkwaɪə] Chor *4*
church [tʃɜːtʃ] Kirche *4*; **go to church** in die Kirche gehen *18*
cinema [ˈsɪnəmə] Kino *11*; **go to the cinema** ins Kino gehen *12*
city [ˈsɪti] Großstadt *9*
class [klɑːs] Kurs, Klasse *8*; **go to a class** einen Kurs besuchen *16*
climate [ˈklaɪmət] Klima *19*
club [klʌb] Klub, Verein *4*
coach [kəʊtʃ] (Reise-)Bus *4*
coast [kəʊst] Küste *21*
code [kəʊd] Vorwahl(nummer) *24*
coffee [ˈkɒfi] Kaffee *6*
cold [kəʊld] kalt *13*; Kälte *19*
college [ˈkɒlɪdʒ] Institut; College *12*

Cologne [kəˈləʊn] Köln *1*
come [kʌm] kommen *2*
concert [ˈkɒnsət] Konzert *18*
cook [kʊk] kochen *18*
cornflakes [ˈkɔːnfleɪks] Cornflakes *17*
countryside [ˈkʌntrisaɪd] Landschaft *11*
couple [ˈkʌpl] Ehepaar *8*
course [kɔːs]; **of course** natürlich *7*
cousin [ˈkʌzn] Cousin/e *2*

d

daughter [ˈdɔːtə] Tochter *2*
daughter-in-law [ˈdɔːtər ɪn lɔː] Schwiegertochter *4*
day [deɪ] Tag *17*
dear [dɪə]; **Oh dear!** Oh je! Oh schade! *13*
different [ˈdɪfrənt] anders *18*
difficult [ˈdɪfɪkəlt] schwierig *22*
dinner [ˈdɪnə] (festliches) Abendessen *14*; **have dinner** zu Abend essen *16*
divorced [dɪˈvɔːst] geschieden *13*
do [duː] tun, machen, unternehmen *11*; **do sport** Sport machen/treiben *18*
doesn't [dʌznt]; **doesn't like** mag nicht *19*
dog [dɒg] Hund *13*
don't [dəʊnt]; **I don't eat …** ich esse nicht *17*
double [ˈdʌbl] Doppel-, doppelt *24*
dress [dres] Kleid *8*
drink [drɪŋk] Getränk *12*; trinken *17*; **go for a drink** etwas trinken gehen *12*

e

early [ˈɜːli] früh *16*
east [iːst] Osten *9*; **in the east of** im Osten von *9*; **East Germany** Ostdeutschland *9*; **east of** östlich von *9*
eat [iːt] essen *17*
egg [eg] Ei *17*
eight [eɪt] acht *8*
eighty [ˈeɪti] achtzig *9*
eleven [ɪˈlevn] elf *8*
else [els]; **What else?** Was sonst (noch)? *11*
email [ˈiːmeɪl] E-Mail *18*
England [ˈɪŋglənd] England *1*
English [ˈɪŋglɪʃ] englisch; Englisch; **English class** Englischkurs *4*
Englishman [ˈɪŋglɪʃmən] Engländer *8*
Englishwoman [ˈɪŋglɪʃwʊmən] Engländerin *8*
evening [ˈiːvnɪŋ] Abend *6*; **Good evening.** Guten Abend. *6*; **in the evening** am Abend, abends *14*
every [ˈevri] jede/r/s *19*
Excuse me … [ɪkˈskjuːz mi] Entschuldigen Sie … *3*

f

family [ˈfæməli] Familie *12*
famous [ˈfeɪməs] berühmt; bedeutend *11*
far [fɑː] weit *9*; **far away** weit weg *21*
fat [fæt] dick *7*
few [fjuː]; **a few** ein paar *24*
fifteen [ˌfɪfˈtiːn] fünfzehn *8*
fifty [ˈfɪfti] fünfzig *9*
fine [faɪn] gut (so) *6*; (ganz) in Ordnung *13*
finish [ˈfɪnɪʃ] aufhören *16*; austrinken, leer machen *23*; **finish work** aufhören zu arbeiten *16*
first name [ˈfɜːst neɪm] Vorname *3*
fish [fɪʃ] Fisch *17*
five [faɪv] fünf *8*
fly [flaɪ] fliegen *24*
football [ˈfʊtbɔːl] Fußball *11*; **football club** Fußballverein *12*; **football team** Fußballmannschaft *11*
for [fɔː] für *13*; **for a few days** ein paar Tage (lang) *24*; **for breakfast** zum Frühstück *17*
forty [ˈfɔːti] vierzig *9*
four [fɔː] vier *8*
fourteen [ˌfɔːˈtiːn] vierzehn *8*
France [frɑːns] Frankreich *1*
free time [ˌfriː ˈtaɪm] Freizeit *16*
French [frentʃ] französisch; Französisch *3*
Friday [ˈfraɪdeɪ] Freitag *16*
friend [frend] Freund/in, Bekannte/r *2*
from [frəm] von, her, aus *1*
fruit [fruːt] Obst *17*
full [fʊl] voll *16*
full-time [ˌfʊl ˈtaɪm] Vollzeit, ganztags *16*
funny [ˈfʌni] lustig, komisch *13*

g

garden [ˈgɑːdn] Garten *16*
German [ˈdʒɜːmən] deutsch; Deutsch; Deutsch/e/r *2*
Germany [ˈdʒɜːməni] Deutschland *1*
get [get] werden *19*; **get on** sich verstehen, miteinander auskommen *22*; **get up** aufstehen *16*
girl [gɜːl] Mädchen *13*
girlfriend [ˈgɜːlfrend] Freundin *2*
go [gəʊ] gehen; fahren *4*; **go for a drink** etwas trinken gehen *12*; **go for a meal** essen gehen *12*; **go for a walk** spazieren gehen *18*; **go hiking** wandern gehen *18*; **go shopping** einkaufen gehen *12*; **go skiing** Ski fahren gehen *18*; **go to a class** einen Kurs besuchen *16*; **go to bed** ins Bett gehen *16*; **go to church** in die Kirche gehen *18*; **go to the cinema** ins Kino gehen *12*; **go to the theatre** ins Theater gehen *12*; **go windsurfing** windsurfen gehen *18*
godchild [ˈgɒdtʃaɪld] Patenkind *2*
good [gʊd] gut *3*; **Good morning/afternoon/evening.** Guten Morgen/Tag/Abend. *6*; **have a good breakfast** gut/reichhaltig frühstücken *17*
goodbye [ˌgʊdˈbaɪ] auf Wiedersehen *4*
good-looking [ˌgʊdˈlʊkɪŋ] gut aussehend *7*
grandchildren [ˈgrændtʃɪldrən] Enkelkinder *13*

granddaughter ['grænddɔːtə] Enkeltochter *2*
grandson ['grændsʌn] Enkelsohn *2*
gymnastics [dʒɪm'næstɪks] Gymnastik *16*

h

half [hɑːf] halb; Hälfte *14*; eight and a half achteinhalb *14*; half past seven halb acht *14*
ham [hæm] Schinken *17*
happy ['hæpi] glücklich *22*
has [hæz] (mit he, she, it) hat *13*
hat [hæt] Hut *22*; in that hat mit dem Hut *22*
have [hæv] haben *2*; essen, trinken *17*; have a holiday (einen) Urlaub machen *19*; have bread Brot essen *17*; have breakfast frühstücken *16*; have dinner/supper/lunch zu Abend/Mittag essen *16*; have tea Tee trinken *17*; have to müssen *24*
he [hiː] er *2*; he's (he is) er ist *2*
heat [hiːt] Hitze *19*
hello [hə'ləʊ] Hallo, guten Tag *1*
help [help] helfen *23*
her [hɜː] ihr/e *2*; sie, ihr *22*
here [hɪə] hier *4*; Here you are. Bitte schön/sehr. *7*
hiking ['haɪkɪŋ] Wandern *18*; go hiking wandern gehen *18*; hiking club Wanderverein *4*
him [hɪm] ihn, ihm *22*
his [hɪz] sein/e *2*
holiday ['hɒlədeɪ] Urlaub *19*; have a holiday (einen) Urlaub machen *19*
home [həʊm] Heim, Zuhause *17*; at home zu Hause
hot [hɒt] heiß; warm *13*
hotel [həʊ'tel] Hotel *4*
hour ['aʊə] Stunde *14*
house [haʊs] Haus *11*
housewife ['haʊswaɪf] Hausfrau *16*
how [haʊ] wie *6*; How are you? Wie geht es dir/euch/Ihnen? *6*; How many? Wie viele? *8*
hundred ['hʌndrəd]; (a/one hundred) (ein)hundert *9*
husband ['hʌzbənd] Ehemann *2*

i

I [aɪ] ich *1*; I'm (I am) ich bin *1*
idea [aɪ'dɪə] Idee *19*
in [ɪn] in *1*; in English auf Englisch *4*; in the afternoon am Nachmittag, nachmittags *17*; in the evening am Abend, abends *16*; in the morning am Morgen, morgens *16*
instant coffee ['ɪnstənt kɒfi] Pulverkaffee, löslicher Kaffee *17*
instead of [ɪn'sted əv] anstatt; anstelle von *14*
interesting ['ɪntrəstɪŋ] interessant *11*
is [ɪz] ist *1*; isn't ist nicht *6*
it [ɪt] es *3*
Italian [ɪ'tæliən] italienisch; Italienisch *3*
Italy ['ɪtəli] Italien *1*

j

jacket ['dʒækɪt] Jacke, Jackett *22*
jam [dʒæm] Marmelade *17*
juice [dʒuːs] Saft *6*
just [dʒʌst] gerade, im Moment *12*; just now gerade im Moment *12*

k

kilometre ['kɪləmiːtə] Kilometer *9*
know [nəʊ] wissen *12*; kennen *19*

l

last [lɑːst] letzte/r/s *6*; last night letzte Nacht; gestern Abend *6*
late [leɪt] (zu) spät, verspätet *13*
later [leɪt] später *4*
leave [liːv] (ab)fahren; verlassen *14*
let [let] lassen *8*; Let me see. Lass(t) / Lassen Sie mal sehen. *8*; Let's … Lass(t) uns / Lassen Sie uns … *19*
letter ['letə] Brief *18*
like [laɪk] wie *12*; mögen, gern essen, trinken *17*; like best am liebsten haben/mögen *19*; What's … like? Wie ist …? *19*; Would you like (to)…? Möchten Sie / Möchtest du / Möchtet ihr …? *16*
listen ['lɪsn]; listen to music Musik hören *16*; listen to the radio Radio hören *16*
little ['lɪtl]; a little ein wenig, ein bisschen *3*
live [lɪv] wohnen, leben *9*
London ['lʌndn] London *1*
look [lʊk] (hin)sehen, (hin)schauen *22*; look at ansehen, anschauen *22*; look for suchen *23*
lot [lɒt]; a lot viel; sehr *18*; a lot of viel/e *11*
love [lʌv] lieben; I'd love to … Ich würde sehr gern … *24*
lovely ['lʌvli] schön, herrlich *12*
lucky ['lʌki]; be lucky Glück haben *22*
lunch [lʌntʃ] Mittagessen *14*; after lunch nach dem Mittagessen *18*; have lunch zu Mittag essen *16*

m

make [meɪk] machen, anfertigen, herstellen *18*; make a cake einen Kuchen backen *18*
man [mæn] Mann *7*
many ['meni] viele *8*
market ['mɑːkɪt] Markt *19*
married ['mærid] verheiratet *7*
me [miː] mich *3*
meal [miːl] Mahlzeit, Essen *12*; go for a meal essen gehen *12*
mean [miːn] meinen *17*
medium-sized ['miːdiəmsaɪzd] mittelgroß *9*
meet [miːt] kennen lernen; treffen; begegnen *1*
member ['membə] Mitglied *4*; a member of a club Mitglied in einem Verein *4*
men [men] Mehrzahl von man *8*
middle ['mɪdl] Mitte *9*

milk [mɪlk] Milch *6*
mind [maɪnd]; **I don't mind ...** Mir macht ... nichts aus. / Ich habe nichts gegen ... *19*
minute ['mɪnɪt] Minute *14*
miss [mɪs] vermissen *22*
modern ['mɒdn] modern *11*
moment ['məʊmənt] Moment, Augenblick *23*; **at the moment** im Moment, im Augenblick *23*
Monday ['mʌndeɪ] Montag *16*; **on Monday** am Montag, montags *16*
month [mʌnθ] Monat *21*
morning ['mɔːnɪŋ] Morgen *6*; **in the morning** am Morgen, morgens *14*; **Good morning.** Guten Morgen. *6*
mountain ['maʊntɪn] Berg *18*
much [mʌtʃ] viel *6*
muesli ['mjuːzli] Müsli *17*
Munich ['mjuːnɪk] München *1*
museum [mjuːˈzɪəm] Museum *4*
music ['mjuːzɪk] Musik *16*
must [mʌst] müssen *4*
my [maɪ] mein/e *1*

n
name [neɪm] Name *1*; **What's your name?** Wie heißen Sie? *3*; **My name's (name is) ...** Mein Name ist ... / Ich heiße ... *1*; **first name** Vorname *3*
near [nɪə] in der Nähe von, nahe (bei) *1*
nearby ['nɪəbaɪ] in der Nähe, nahebei *21*
neighbour ['neɪbə] Nachbar/in *4*
nephew ['nefjuː] Neffe *2*
never ['nevə] nie *16*
New England [njuː 'ɪŋglənd] Neuengland *21*
new [njuː] neu *11*
newspaper ['njuːspeɪpə] Zeitung *18*
next [nekst] nächste/r/s *14*; **next to** neben *7*
nice [naɪs] nett, schön *1*; **Nice to meet you.** Nett, Sie kennen zu lernen. *1*; **nice and warm** schön warm *19*
niece [niːs] Nichte *2*
night [naɪt] Nacht *6*; **last night** gestern Abend, letzte Nacht *6*; **night club** Nachtclub *11*
nine [naɪn] neun *8*
ninety ['naɪnti] neunzig *9*
no [nəʊ] nein *1*; kein/e *13*
noisy ['nɔɪzi] laut *13*
normal ['nɔːml] normal, gewöhnlich, üblich *17*
north [nɔːθ] Norden *9*; **in the north of** im Norden von *9*; **north of** nördlich von *9*
not [nɒt] nicht *1*
now [naʊ] jetzt, nun *4*
number ['nʌmbə] Nummer, Zahl, Ziffer *23*

o
o'clock [əˈklɒk]; **10 o'clock** 10 Uhr *14*; **at 11 o'clock** um 11 Uhr *14*
of [əv] von *3*; **a member of a club** Mitglied in einem Verein *4*; **of course** natürlich *7*
often ['ɒfn] oft, meistens *16*
oh [əʊ] ach, oh (je) *2*
OK [ˌəʊˈkeɪ] OK, okay, in Ordnung *4*
old [əʊld] alt *7*
on [ɒn]; **on Monday** am Montag, montags *16*
once [wʌns] einmal, ein Mal *21*; **once a year** einmal im Jahr *21*
one [wʌn] eins *8*
only ['əʊnli] nur *17*
or [ɔː] oder *6*
originally [əˈrɪdʒənəli] ursprünglich *9*
our ['aʊə] unser/e *6*
over there [ˌəʊvə 'ðeə] da drüben *2*
Oxford ['ɒksfəd] Oxford *1*

p
pack [pæk] packen *23*
pair of trousers [ˌpeər əv 'traʊzəz] Hose *22*
paper ['peɪpə] Papier *24*; **piece of paper** Blatt Papier *24*
park [pɑːk] Park(anlage) *11*
part [pɑːt] Teil *21*
partner ['pɑːtnə] Partner/in *2*
part-time [ˌpɑːt'taɪm] Teilzeit *16*
past [pɑːst]; **past seven** nach sieben *14*
people ['piːpl] Leute, Personen *7*
pepper ['pepə] Pfeffer *7*
perhaps [pəˈhæps] vielleicht, eventuell *12*
phone [fəʊn] telefonieren *18*
phone number ['fəʊn nʌmbə] Telefonnummer *24*
photo ['fəʊtəʊ] Foto *12*
piece [piːs] Blatt, Stück *24*
place [pleɪs] Ort, Platz, Stelle *9*
plane [pleɪn] Flugzeug *14*
please [pliːz] bitte *6*; **Yes, please.** Ja bitte. / Ja gerne. *6*
pm [ˌpiː 'em] (post meridiem) nachmittags, abends *14*
postcard ['pəʊstkɑːd] Postkarte *21*
postcode ['pəʊstkəʊd] Postleitzahl *24*
pretty ['prɪti] hübsch *22*
problem ['prɒbləm] Problem *22*
pronunciation [prəˌnʌnsi'eɪʃn] Aussprache *8*
pub [pʌb] Pub, Kneipe, Gaststätte *11*
pullover ['pʊləʊvə] Pullover *8*

q
quarter ['kwɔːtə] Viertel *14*
quiet ['kwaɪət] ruhig *18*
quite [kwaɪt] ziemlich *21*

r
radio ['reɪdiəʊ] Radio *16*
rain [reɪn] Regen; regnen *19*
rather ['rɑːðə]; **I'd rather not** (ich würde) lieber nicht ... *19*; **or rather** das heißt, oder eigentich *23*
read [riːd] lesen *16*
really ['rɪəli] wirklich, tatsächlich *2*; eigentlich *11*

relative ['relətɪv] Verwandte/r *13*
remember [rɪ'membə] sich erinnern (an); an … denken *22*
restaurant ['restrɒnt] Restaurant *4*
retired [rɪ'taɪəd] im Ruhestand, pensioniert *16*
right [raɪt] richtig *1*; all right in Ordnung *23*
river ['rɪvə] Fluss *11*
roll [rəʊl] Brötchen *17*
room [ruːm] Zimmer, Raum *23*

s

salt [sɔːlt] Salz *7*
Saturday ['sætədeɪ] Samstag, Sonnabend *16*
sausage ['sɒsɪdʒ] Wurst *17*
say [seɪ] sagen *8*
see [siː] sehen *8*; See you later. Bis später. *4*
seven ['sevn] sieben *8*
seventy [ˌsevn'tiːn] siebzig *9*
shall [ʃəl] sollen *19*
she [ʃiː] sie *2*; she's (she is) sie ist *2*
ship [ʃɪp] Schiff *14*
shirt [ʃɜːt] Hemd *22*
shop [ʃɒp] Geschäft, Laden *11*
shopkeeper ['ʃɒp kiːpə] Ladenbesitzer/in *21*
shopping ['ʃɒpɪŋ] Einkaufen; go shopping einkaufen gehen *12*
short [ʃɔːt] kurz *7*
sing [sɪŋ] singen *23*; he's singing to her er singt ihr (gerade) etwas vor *23*
single ['sɪŋgl] allein stehend, ledig *7*
sister ['sɪstə] Schwester *2*
six [sɪks] sechs *8*
sixteen ['sɪkstiːn] sechzehn *8*
sixty ['sɪksti] sechzig *9*
skiing ['skiːɪŋ] Skifahren *18*; go skiing Ski fahren gehen *18*
skirt [skɜːt] Rock *22*
slim [slɪm] schlank *7*
small [smɔːl] klein *9*
smart [smɑːt] schick *22*
snow [snəʊ] schneien *19*
so [səʊ] so *6*; also *13*
some [sʌm] etwas *6*; einige, ein paar *11*
sometimes ['sʌmtaɪmz] manchmal *16*
son [sʌn] Sohn *2*
son-in-law ['sʌn ɪn lɔː] Schwiegersohn *4*
sorry ['sɒri]; I'm sorry. Es/Das tut mir Leid. *6*; Entschuldigung. *23*
south [saʊθ] Süden *9*; in the south of im Süden von *9*; south of südlich von *9*; south-west of südwestlich von *9*
souvenir [ˌsuːvə'nɪə] Reiseandenken, Souvenir *19*
Spain [speɪn] Spanien *1*
Spanish ['spænɪʃ] spanisch; Spanisch *3*
speak [spiːk] sprechen *3*
spell [spel] buchstabieren *24*
sport [spɔːt] Sport *18*; do sport Sport machen/treiben *18*; sports centre Sportzentrum *11*; sports club Sportverein *4*

spring [sprɪŋ] Frühling *18*
start [stɑːt] anfangen, beginnen *16*; start work anfangen zu arbeiten *16*
stay [steɪ] bleiben; übernachten *22*
stop [stɒp] anhalten, stoppen; aufhören *19*
street [striːt] Straße *3*
sugar ['ʃʊgə] Zucker *7*
summer ['sʌmə] Sommer *18*
sun [sʌn] Sonne *19*
Sunday ['sʌndeɪ] Sonntag *16*
supper ['sʌpə] Abendessen *16*; have supper zu Abend essen *16*
sure [ʃʊə] sicher *21*
surname ['sɜːneɪm] Familienname *3*
swimming pool ['swɪmɪŋ puːl] Schwimmbad *11*
Switzerland ['swɪtsələnd] die Schweiz *1*

t

tall [tɔːl] groß (gewachsen) *7*
Tangier [tæn'dʒɪə] Tanger *14*
tea [tiː] Tee *6*; tea Teezeit *14*; have tea Tee trinken *17*
teacher ['tiːtʃə] Lehrer/in *4*
team [tiːm] Mannschaft *11*
telephone ['telɪfəʊn] Telefon *24*; telephone number Telefonnummer *24*
tell [tel] erzählen *11*; Tell me. Sagen Sie/Sag mal. *7*
ten [ten] zehn *8*
thank you; thanks. ['θæŋk ju, θæŋks] danke *6*
that [ðæt] das *1*; jene/r/s (dort); diese/r/s (hier) *22*
the [ðə, ðiː] der, die, das *1*
theatre ['θɪətə] Theater *11*; go to the theatre ins Theater gehen *12*
their [ðeə] ihr/e *7*
them [ðem] sie *22*
then [ðən] dann *18*
there [ðeə] da, dort; dorthin *2*; there's (there is) es gibt *11*; there are es gibt/sind *8*;
they [ðeɪ] sie *4*
thing [θɪŋ] Ding, Sache *22*
think [θɪŋk] meinen, glauben *21*
thirteen [ˌθɜː'tiːn] dreizehn *8*
thirty ['θɜːti] dreißig *9*
this [ðɪs] dies, das; diese/r/s *3*; this morning/afternoon/evening heute Morgen/Nachmittag/Abend *14*
three [θriː] drei *8*
Thursday ['θɜːzdeɪ] Donnerstag *16*
time [taɪm] Zeit *14*; Mal *21*; three times dreimal, drei Mal *21*; What is the time? / What time is it? Wie spät ist es? *14*
tired ['taɪəd] müde *7*
to [tə, tʊ, tuː] zu *1*; to bed ins Bett *16*; to eleven vor elf *14*; write to … an … schreiben *18*
today [tə'deɪ] heute *6*
tomorrow [tə'mɒrəʊ] morgen *19*
too [tuː] zu *6*; auch *11*
tour group ['tʊə gruːp] Reisegruppe *4*

town [taʊn] Stadt *3*
train [treɪn] Zug, Eisenbahn *14*
trousers ['traʊzəz]; **pair of trousers** Hose *22*
Tuesday ['tjuːzdeɪ] Dienstag *16*
TV [ˌtiː 'viː] Fernsehen *16*
twelve [twelv] zwölf *8*
twenty ['twenti] zwanzig *8*
twice [twaɪs] zweimal, zwei Mal *21*
twin town [twɪn' taʊn] Partnerstadt *4*
two [tuː] zwei *8*
typical ['tɪpɪkl] typisch *18*

u

understand [ʌndə'stænd] verstehen *21*
United States [juˌnaɪtɪd 'steɪts] Vereinigte Staaten *1*
university [ˌjuːnɪ'vɜːsəti] Universität *12*
unusual [ʌn'juːʒʊəl] ungewöhnlich *22*
up auf, hoch *17*
us [ʌs] uns *22*
USA [juː es 'eɪ] USA *1*
usually ['juːʒuəli] normalerweise; gewöhnlich *16*

v

very ['veri] sehr *6*
via ['vaɪə] über *24*
Vienna [vi'enə] Wien *1*
village ['vɪlɪdʒ] Dorf *9*
visit ['vɪzɪt] besuchen *12*

w

walk [wɔːk] Spaziergang *18*; **go for a walk** spazieren gehen, einen Spaziergang machen *18*
want (to) [wɒnt tə] wollen *19*
warm [wɔːm] warm *13*
watch [wɒtʃ] (Armband-)Uhr *8*
watch TV [wɒtʃ ˌtiːˈviː] fernsehen *16*
water ['wɔːtə] Wasser *6*
we [wiː] wir *4*
weather ['weðə] Wetter *19*; **What's the weather like?** Wie ist das Wetter? *19*
Wednesday ['wenzdeɪ] Mittwoch *16*
week [wiːk] Woche *21*
weekend [ˌwiːk'end] Wochenende *18*; **at the weekend** am Wochenende *18*
welcome ['welkəm]; **You're welcome.** Keine Ursache. / Bitte sehr/schön. *7*
well [wel] nun *4*; gut *21*; **I'm not very well.** Mir geht es nicht (sehr) gut. *6*
west [west] Westen *9*; **in the west of** im Westen von *9*; **west of** westlich von *9*
what [wɒt] was *3*; **What about …?** Was ist mit …?; Wie ist es mit …? *16*; **What's … in English?** Wie heißt … auf Englisch? *4*; **What's your name?** Wie heißen Sie? *3*; **What's your telephone number?** Wie ist Ihre Telefonnummer? *24*; **What time is it? / What is the time?** Wie spät ist es? *14*; **What time will dinner be?** Um wie viel Uhr wird das Abendessen sein? *14*; **What's … like?** Wie ist …? *19*
when [wen] wann *14*; wenn *17*
where [weə] wo, wohin *1*; **Where are you from?** Woher kommen/sind Sie? *1*
which [wɪtʃ] welche/r/s *23*
who [huː] wer *7*
wife [waɪf] Ehefrau *2*
will [wɪl] werden *14*
windsurfing ['wɪndsɜːfɪŋ] Windsurfen *18*; **go windsurfing** windsurfen gehen *18*
wine [waɪn] Wein *6*
winter ['wɪntə] Winter *18*
with [wɪð, wɪθ] mit *4*; **with (their) supper** zum Abendessen *17*
wives [waɪvz] Mehrzahl von **wife** *8*
woman ['wʊmən] Frau *8*
women ['wɪmɪn] Mehrzahl von **woman** *8*
word [wɜːd] Wort *24*
work [wɜːk] Arbeit; arbeiten *16*; **finish work** aufhören zu arbeiten *16*; **start work** anfangen zu arbeiten *16*
Would you like (to) …? [ˌwəd juː 'laɪk tə] Möchtest du / Möchtet ihr / Möchten Sie …? *6*
write [raɪt] schreiben *18*; **write to** an … schreiben *18*

y

year [jɪə] Jahr *19*
yes [jes] ja *1*
you [juː] du, ihr, Sie *1*; man *18*
young [jʌŋ] jung *7*
your [jɔː] dein/e, euer, eure, Ihr/e *2*

z

Zurich ['zʊərɪk] Zürich *1*

Lösungsschlüssel Units

Frei gestellte Aufgaben sind in diesem Lösungsschlüssel nicht aufgeführt.

Unit 1

1 1, 4, 2, 3

2 B 'm, are, Are   B are   B 's   B 'm, 's
     A 'm, 'm   A are   A Are

3 2 Where are you from?
     3 Is your name Inge?
     4 Are you from London?
     5 Is Bonn near Cologne?
     6 Is Inge from Bonn?

4 1 Where are you from?
     2 Are you from the United States?
     3 Yes, that's right.
     4 I'm (am) from Germany.
     5 My name's (is) Inge.

Unit 2

1 1 husband   3 cousin   5 have   7 brother   9 daughter
     2 grandson   4 Germany   6 sister 8 friend

2 2 she   3 he   4 she

3 1 He's   2 His   3 He's   4 His   5 He's

4 she's, her, Her, he's, His

5 1 I have a daughter in the USA.
     2 Really?
     3 My son's (is) in Bavaria, near Munich.
     4 Come and meet my friend Mary.

Unit 3

1 2 C, 3 A, 4 E, 5 B

2 2 … my daughter. Her name is Sonia.
     3 This is her husband. His name is Tony.
     4 And this is my grandson. His name is Philip.
     5 This is my granddaughter. Her name is Stella.
     6 This is my son. His name is Kevin.
     7 And this is my son's girlfriend. Her name is Carmen.

3 1 French   2 German   3 Italian   4 Spanish   5 English

4 1 Where's, It's   3 Where's   5 What's, It's
     2 What's, It's   4 Where's, It's

Unit 4

1 1 am   3 is   5 is   7 are
     2 is   4 are   6 is   8 is

3 Linkes Bild: They're grandfather and granddaughter. She's with her grandfather. He's from the USA.
Rechtes Bild: She's his mother. They're from Germany. He's her son.

4 2 E, 3 G, 4 C, 5 F, 6 D, 7 B

Unit 6

1 Excuse me. (Are you David Barker?)
No, I'm afraid (not. David is in the restaurant.)

2 1 Yes, she is.   4 No, she isn't.
     2 No, she isn't.   5 Yes, she is.
     3 Yes, she is.

4 2 Good morning. How are you today?
     3 I'm fine thanks. And you?
     4 Fine thanks. Would you like some coffee?
     5 Yes, please. How is your husband?
     6 He isn't very well, I'm afraid. He's in the hotel.
     7 Oh, I'm sorry.

5 1 How are you?   5 No, thank you.
     2 Fine, thanks.   6 I'm not (very) well.
     3 Would you like some coffee? – Yes, please. 7 Oh, I'm sorry.
     4 Would you like some tea? Or water?

Unit 7

1a 2 No, they aren't.   3 Yes, she is.   4 No, he isn't.

2 Menschen: husband, member, wife, neighbour, teacher
     Gebäude: shop, bar, church, hotel, restaurant, museum
     Essen: bread, butter, salt, sugar, pepper
     Getränke: coffee, juice, milk, water, tea

3 MELANIE Black, Tony's sister (wife), In a restaurant in Oxford
                                       (In the museum with her daughter)
     TINA Washington, Tony's wife (sister), In the museum with her daughter
                                       (In a restaurant in Oxford)
     GEORGE Street, Tony's son-in-law from Chicago, In bed in the Plaza Hotel
     HELEN Street, Tony's daughter, In a museum in New York

Unit 8

1a 2 two watches
     3 eight men and seven women
     4 Three of my friends and their wives are members …
     5 two evening classes
     6 names and addresses of six hotels
     7 fifteen pullovers and twelve blouses

2 1 an, a, an, –   3 A, a, an
     2 a, an, an, an   4 a, an

3 B Ten and twelve is twenty-two.
     C Seven and four is eleven.
     D Fifteen and five is twenty.

4

```
            T
    T H R E E
    W   N I N E
F I V E   G
    L   O H   F
S E V E N   T W O
I   E   E       U
X           R
```

Unit 9

1 2 St Albans is about thirty-five kilometres north-west of London.
3 Canterbury is about eighty-five kilometres south-east of London.
4 Colchester is about eighty kilometres north-east of London.
5 Guildford is about forty-five kilometres south-west of London.
6 Henley is about fifty-five kilometres west of London.
7 Brighton is about seventy-five kilometres south of London.

2a Canterbury

4 1 Where are you from in Germany?
2 We live in Euskirchen.
3 It's a medium-sized town.
4 It's about 30 kilometres east of Munich.
5 I'm from Mannheim originally.

Unit 11

1 1 there are   3 there is   5 there is   7 there are   9 there is
2 There is   4 There is   6 There are   8 There are

2 There is some … butter, milk, tea, toast

There isn't any … bread, coffee, jam, juice, sugar, water

3 1 about   5 go   9 else
2 Let   6 Excuse   10 really
3 too   7 to
4 of   8 How

4 1 Tell me about Euskirchen.   4 There aren't a lot of good shops.
2 What is there to do and see?   5 There's beautiful countryside.
3 What else is there?

Unit 12

1 1 Yes, there is.   4 No, there isn't.   7 No, there isn't.
2 No, there isn't.   5 Yes, there are.   8 No, there aren't.
3 Yes, there is.   6 Yes. there is.   9 Yes, there are.

3 1 some.
2 any – No, there aren't, I'm afraid.
3 some – Sorry, the photos are all in my hotel.
4 some – Yes, please.
5 any – No, sorry. But there is some nice wine.
6 any – No, I'm afraid not. We're all from Austria.

Unit 13

1 Senkrecht:
1 am	3 too	8 near	10 lot
2 over	7 one	9 with	13 else

Waagerecht:
1 about	5 of	9 Where	12 next
4 from	6 for	11 All	14 to

3 Reihenfolge von oben nach unten, linke Spalte zuerst: 5, 3, 1, 2, 4, 6

4
man	woman	people
boy	wife	children
husband	girl	couple

5
1 He's married and has two children.
2 She's divorced.
3 How old are your grandchildren?
4 My granddaughters are five and three.

Unit 14

1
1 (a) quarter past seven
2 (a) quarter to eight
3 half past eight
4 five to nine
5 ten past eleven
6 half past one
7 twenty-five to five
8 twenty-five past five

2
2 What time will the coach to Oxford leave?
3 When will we arrive there?
4 What time will we meet again?
5 When will lunch be?

4
1 breakfast, lunch, tea, dinner
2 twenty-five past two, half past two, twenty-five to three, half past three
3 awful, OK, lovely, very beautiful

5
1 Excuse me. What time is it?
2 When will the ship leave again? – At half past seven.
3 So how much time will we have there? – Eight and a half hours.
4 What time will dinner be this evening?

Unit 16

1 I get up at seven o'clock. Then I have breakfast – cornflakes, toast and tea. I leave the house at half past eight and start work at nine. I work full-time. I have lunch at one o'clock in our canteen, and I finish work at half past four. I often go shopping – there's a shop near my house. I have supper at six or half past six – it's usually a hot meal. In the evening I read/watch TV or watch TV/read. But on Tuesday I go to a gymnastics class.

2
1 go for a drink
2 go to the Sterling Silver evening class
3 go shopping
4 go to the theatre
5 go for a meal
6 go to the pub
7 go on the river
8 go to a (gymnastics) class
9 go to the cinema
10 go on a train
11 restaurant

3a 2 I have coffee and toast in the morning. / In the morning I have …
3 I always have lunch in town.
4 I go to my choir on Friday. / On Friday I go to … /
5 I finish work at four o'clock. / At four o'clock I …
6 I usually go to bed late.
7 I often watch TV.
8 I never get up early.

Unit 17

1 … so I don't get up very early. … but I don't have a big breakfast … I don't go shopping on Saturday morning … I don't go to the theatre … I don't visit my relatives … but I don't like his wife very much so I don't go there very often.

3
1 yes   5 yes
2 no   6 no
3 no   7 no
4 yes   8 yes

4 **You can eat:** an egg, a cold lunch, a hot meal, some sausages
You can drink: instant coffee, some fruit juice, cold milk, a bottle of wine

Unit 18

1 He works in Munich. In his free time he goes hiking and he goes to concerts. He cooks, too. His wife likes that. Inge's daughter lives in the United States. She works in Boston. In her free time she goes to concerts and watches TV.

2 Then she has breakfast. She leaves the house at 8.30 and starts work at 9.00. She works full-time. She finishes work at 4.30.
Es handelt sich um Ann.

3a BRUNO
He plays cards. / He goes to the pub.
He goes to a cookery class.
He meets his bowling club friends.
INGE
She plays tennis. / She goes hiking.
She goes to an English class.
She meets friends on the internet.
BOTH
They both like wine.
They both speak German and English.

4 Richtige Lösungen: 2 after lunch   4 in   6 to   8 go
                         3 On   5 to bed   7 In

5 1 At the weekend he does a lot of sport.
2 His wife likes music.
3 Then sometimes I read the newspaper.
4 Bavaria is a nice place to live.

Unit 19

1 Chris works full-time, but Monika doesn't work full-time. She only works part-time. Chris speaks German and Monika speaks English. She also speaks Italian, but Chris doesn't speak Italian. In her free time Monika sings in a choir. Chris doesn't sing in a choir, but he does a lot of sport. On Sunday Monika goes to church. But Chris doesn't go to church. Chris likes … Monika doesn't like the summer – she likes the autumn. But she likes …

2
1 doesn't like
2 go
3 don't have
4 go
5 want
6 lives
7 doesn't come
8 don't see
9 likes
10 doesn't want

4
4 in
5 at
6 in
7 on
8 at
9 on

Unit 21

1a
2 Do you watch it every evening?
3 Do you get up late on Sunday?
4 Do you work full-time?

2
2 Austria
3 French
4 English/American
5 Italian
6 Spain

3a
2 How often do they see their daughter?
3 How often do they go to the theatre?
4 How often do they eat fish?
5 How often do they go shopping?
6 How often do they have a holiday?

4
1 Do you often see your family?
2 Do they speak English here?
3 What do you think?
4 I'm sure they understand English.
5 Do you know Boston?

Unit 22

1a
1 No, she doesn't.
2 Yes, she does.
3 Yes, he does.
4 Yes, he does.
5 No, he doesn't.
6 Yes, she does.
7 Yes, she does.
8 Yes, it does.
9 Yes, she does.
10 No, she doesn't.
11 No, he doesn't.
12 No, she doesn't.

2a
2 When does Inge write an email to Anke?
3 When does Inge meet friends for a drink?
4 When does Inge go shopping?
5 When does Inge go to her English class?

3 Senkrecht:
2 my
4 our
5 us
7 them

Waagerecht:
1 him
3 you
6 it
8 us
9 her
10 me

Unit 23

2 B twelve   D forty-six   F thirteen
  C ninety-seven   E fifty-three

4 1 working   3 staying   5 writing   7 going
  2 listening   4 doing   6 drinking

5 1 B I'm / I am working   4 E They're / They are looking
  2 D She's / She is phoning   5 C We're / We are making
  3 A He's / He is cooking

Unit 24

1b 1 F, L, M, N, S   4 I, Y
  2 B, C, D, E, G, P, T, V   5 Q, U, W
  3 A, H, J, K

2 1 What   3 Who   5 What   7 What
  2 How   4 What   6 How

3 Reihenfolge von oben nach unten:
  5, 2, 1, 4, 8, 3, 7, 6, 9

4 1 D, 2 C, 3 B, 4 A

5 Senkrecht: 1 love   3 code   6 post
            2 stay   5 funny   10 to

  Waagerecht: 1 last   6 phone   9 not
            4 via   7 your   11 fly
            5 few   8 spell

Hinweis für den Kursleiter / die Kursleiterin

Unit 7, Exercise 3 (Eine mögliche Variante ist in Klammern angegeben.)

First name	Surname	Who is it?	Where is he/she now?
MELANIE	Black	Tony's sister (wife)	In a restaurant in Oxford
TINA	Washington	Tony's wife (sister)	In the museum with her daughter (In a restaurant in Oxford)
GEORGE	Street	Tony's son-in-law	In bed in the Plaza Hotel in Chicago
HELEN	Street	Tony's daughter	In a museum in New York

Lösungsschlüssel Home Practice

Unit 1
1 1 is 3 am 5 Are, am
2 are 4 am, am

2 2 No, I'm not. 4 No, I'm not.
3 Yes, I am. 5 Yes, I am

Unit 2
1 my 3 (you) 5 He's 7 Her
2 I'm 4 you 6 His 8 She's

Unit 3
A Excuse me. Can you speak English?
B Yes, I can. A little.
A Oh good. What's the name of this street?
B It's Lenzstraße.
A Lenzstraße. Is that right?
B Yes, that's right.

Unit 4
1 bar, hotel, restaurant, museum

2 2 Her husband's first name is Bruno.
3 He is a member of a bowling club.
4 What's the name of the club?
5 The address of my hotel is Museum Street, London.
6 The name of my choir is Allegro Vivace.

3 in, of, near, with, from

4a 2 Hello. (die einzige Begrüßung)
3 street (die anderen drei bezeichnen Menschen)

4b 1 bar/museum usw. (es sind alles Gebäude/Einrichtungen)
2 son/daughter/grandson/granddaughter/brother/sister/cousin/niece/nephew usw. (es sind alles Verwandte)
3 German/Italian/Spanish (es sind alles Sprachen)

Unit 6
1 Waagerecht: 1 His, His 2 my 4 our
Senkrecht: 1 her 3 your

2 1 Goodbye. (der einzige Abschiedsgruß)
2 Yes, please. (die anderen drei sind Antworten auf die Frage *How are you?*)
3 wine (das einzige alkoholische Getränk)

Unit 7
1 They're, They're, their, their, They're, their

2 2 E 6 F/D
3 A 7 D/F
4 B 8 G
5 H

3 1 Yes, they are. 4 Yes, they are.
2 No, they aren't. 5 No, they aren't.
3 Yes, they are.

4 1 Where 2 What 3 Who 4 How

Unit 8
Männer: (brothers,) Englishmen, grandsons, husbands
Frauen: (daughters,) daughters-in-law, sisters, wives
Männer und Frauen: (friends,) Germans, members, neighbours, teachers

Unit 9
1 is ('s)
2 is not (isn't), is ('s)
3 are, are not (aren't)
4 am not ('m not), am ('m)
5 are not (aren't), are ('re)

Unit 11
1 some, any
2 a, some
3 some, any
4 any
5 a, a
6 any
7 any, some
8 some, any
9 some

Unit 12
2 Would you like some coffee?
3 Would you like to visit me in Germany?
4 Would you like the butter?
5 Would you like to come and meet Angela?

Unit 13
1 has
2 have
3 has
4 has
5 have
6 has
7 have
8 has
9 has, have

Unit 14
1 The next plane leaves at six o'clock.
2 What time is it?
3 When is the next train?
4 How much time will we have in London?

Unit 16
1 Saturday
2 Sunday
3 Tuesday
4 Thursday
5 Friday
6 Wednesday
7 Monday

Unit 17
2 G We arrive …
3 A They don't live …
4 B I speak …
5 F and I finish …
6 H but I don't like …
7 C but we get up …
8 E I don't like …

Unit 18
1 D live, live
2 A sings, does
3 E speak, speak
4 B works, works
5 C like, go

Unit 19
1 What
2 How
3 How
4 What
5 What
6 How

Unit 21
letter – postcard
far away – nearby
I'm sure – I don't know
often – never
twice – once
stop – start

Unit 22
1
1 does
2 Does
3 does
4 Do
5 do
6 Does
7 doesn't
8 Do
8 don't
10 doesn't

2
1 Glenn
2 Mary
3 Ann
4 Bruno & Inge, Anke & Glenn
5 Ann, Ann's son (Chris) & his wife (Monika)
6 Glenn

Unit 23
2 She's listening to the radio.
3 They're watching TV.
4 She's reading.
5 He's singing.
6 He's cooking.

Quellennachweis

Fotos
Titel: Corbis/Norbert Schäfer

Britain On View: S. 48;
COMSTOCK: S. 43;
Corbis GmbH: S. 43 Angelo Hornak, S. 50 Paul Thompson, S. 58 Chris Lisle, S. 76 Hubert Stadler (3), Ray Juno, S. 82 Richard Klune, Ray Juno, Hubert Stadler;
Corel: S. 47;
F1 online: S. 46 Thomas Nuehnen;
Getty Images: S. 21 Romilly Lockyer;
Hapag-Lloyd Kreuzfahrten GmbH, Hamburg: S. 8, 10;
IFA-Bilderteam: S. 26 Reporters, S. 80 Nägele;
Images.de digital photo GmbH: S. 14 Geoff Williamson;
Schapowalow GmbH & Cie. KG: S. 50 Heaton, S. 51 Brooke;
Stockfood: S. 44 Foodphotography Eising;
Werner Otto Reisefotografie: S. 46

Karten
S. 9, S. 11, S. 42: Carlos Borrell, Berlin